Becoming Married

FAMILY LIVING
IN PASTORAL PERSPECTIVE

FAMILY LIVING IN PASTORAL PERSPECTIVE

BECOMING MARRIED

HERBERT ANDERSON
AND ROBERT COTTON FITE

WESTMINSTER/JOHN KNOX PRESS
LOUISVILLE, KENTUCKY

Book design by Drew Stevens
Cover design by Jeff Tull, Fearless Designs

First edition

Published by Westminster/John Knox Press
Louisville, Kentucky

This book is printed on acid-free paper that meets the American National Standards Institute Z39.48 standard. ∞

PRINTED IN THE UNITED STATES OF AMERICA
9   8   7   6   5   4   3   2   1

Library of Congress Cataloging-in-Publication Data

Anderson, Herbert, 1936–
    Becoming married / Herbert Anderson and Robert Cotton Fite. — 1st ed.
        p.   cm. — (Family living in pastoral perspective)
    ISBN 0–664–25126–9 (acid–free paper)

    1. Marriage—Religious aspects—Christianity.   2. Family—
Religious life.   I. Fite, Robert Cotton.   II. Title.   III. Series:
Anderson, Herbert, 1936–   Family living in pastoral perspective.
BV835.H64   1993
248.8'44—dc20   93–4537

CONTENTS

INTRODUCTION

CILANTRO, DILL, AND THE DUTCH COUNTRYSIDE are an unlikely combination, but for me all three call up images of wedding celebrations. Both of my children were married recently. My daughter's wedding was first. She and her husband planned a wedding around the theme of blessing and personally welcomed everyone who came to the church that afternoon to celebrate the family they intend to become. Each guest received a twenty-five-page booklet of their reflections, favorite quotations, and family stories. The blessings continued as guests enjoyed a Swedish–Puerto Rican meal prepared by the parents. Pungent odors of cilantro and dill filled the hall and symbolized their very distinct heritages. They did forget to cut the cake until some guests had already gone home. No matter. Everybody had a great time.

My son was married in the Netherlands in a civil ceremony in a city hall dating from the sixteenth century. After that event, the wedding company of about sixty traveled by barge for a grand celebration that included reflection on the meaning of love and commitment and the value of family. Their wedding occurred in a circle of family and friends that spans the globe. The death of the bride's favorite uncle on the night before the wedding added a note of sorrow to an occasion otherwise filled with joy. On the day after the wedding, my son and his wife organized a bicycle tour through the Dutch country-side at tulip time as a way of including family and friends in the beginning of their life together.

Like most parents today, we did not *give* our children away but rather blessed them. Family is important for my children but so are their friends. These friends are an increasingly significant part of the public in which our sons and daughters make their commitments to become married. The traditional roles of parents are also changing. Because children live away from home before they marry, marry later, marry more than once, or marry across cultural traditions, the role of parents is less significant.

From being involved with both of my children's weddings, I learned a valuable axiom: *Stay close and stay out.* Conflicts arise in planning for a wedding when parents want to exercise too much influence or control, or when daughters and sons understand the meaning of the ritual differently than their parents do. The wedding is not something parents *give* their children to send them on their way. Nor is it something that the church *does* to validate a relationship. *The wedding is rather a commitment that two people make to each other in the company of family and friends and community and in the presence of God that enhances the process of becoming married.* Understanding the wedding in that way made it is easier for me to stay close and stay out.

This book is being written with an awareness that the process of becoming married is seldom as perfect as the wedding that inaugurates it. Most of the time it is our intent to live together and love the best way we can. The continuing frequency of divorce is a sobering reality that our best is not always enough. For some people marrying today, the multiplication of individual choices and the reluctance to change gender role expectations makes marriage seem like an impossible ideal. Couples with complicated schedules need to settle questions like who cooks or shops, or who will move for the other's career, or who will take the children to Little League. The question who will make a home is often left unanswered: when it is nobody's job, everybody suffers from the neglect. Moreover, because the demands of market societies for individual mobility conflict with the expectations for equality between women and men, marriage seems like an impractical possibility for those with career goals.[1]

Despite all these obstacles, however, people continue to marry. And then they struggle to stay married. Indeed, staying married is as difficult as becoming married, and yet it is worth the struggle. In the midst of working hard, we discover the gifts of love and joy that are life-sustaining. This book is written with the hope that it will provide insight and encouragement not just to those planning to marry but for anyone who wants to understand the process of becoming and being married.

The Aim of the Book

This book is about becoming married, a process that happens over time. The wedding is a transitional event that occurs in the midst of a process that both precedes and follows it. From the beginning, at least as scriptures report it, the task has been the same: *one must leave home in order to get married.* While the ways of leaving home and the images of marriage have changed through the centuries, what is necessary to *become* married has not changed: leaving home. One must be emotionally separated from one's parents in order to become emotionally committed to another person in marriage. Effective differentiation from one's originating family makes commitment to forming a new family possible.

This book is also about the importance of knowing the family legacy we bring to marriage. And it is about understanding the continuing impact of our families of origin on becoming married. Because the process of emotional separation from one's home of origin continues throughout life, cleaving usually begins before leaving is completed. This book is also about preparing for a wedding and the process of bonding that both precedes it and follows it. We need more weddings that wed. Planning a ritual that embodies and anticipates the kind of family the couple would like to create is a significant part of pre-wedding work.

In the previous volume, *Leaving Home,* written with Kenneth R. Mitchell, he and I considered when and how and how long that process ordinarily takes. We also suggested that the freedom to make one's own home is one goal of leaving home. The emphasis on leaving home for the sake of greater self-definition in order to become married is supported by the paradoxical assumption that human beings are at the same time autonomous *and* communal creatures.

If we take seriously the idea that becoming married is a process that takes time, then being married is something couples discover at unexpected moments in the midst of that process.

> Doug and I had lived together for several years before we were married. After the wedding, our life remained about the same. We lived in the same house I had lived in before, and I commuted to my same job. Three years after our wedding, Doug received a job offer that would have meant that I give up a tenured teaching position. Even though he turned down the offer, having to think through giving up my job made me aware of being married in a way that I had not been before. (Sybil)

This book is for those planning to marry, for parents who want to stay close to children marrying but stay out of the process, and for pastors and other ministers who work with couples about to marry. People like Sybil and Doug will also find in this book a framework for understanding how the process of becoming married happens over time. The book will be of benefit to anyone intending to marry or working with people who intend to marry, even though the frame of reference is pastoral.

The major themes of this book are developed in the following way. In chapter 1, the focus is on the shift from a private to a public commitment during courtship as a continuation of the process of leaving home. Chapter 2 is on understanding the legacy we receive from our families of origin in order to be self-conscious about its influence in forming a family. Chapter 3 is about planning a wedding that will anticipate the kind of family that the marrying couple would like to become. In chapter 4, we examine three ordinary issues in becoming married that are intensified because of the nature of the relationship or the circumstances of wedding. Chapter 5 is about major themes in the first years of marriage and how the church's post-wedding pastoral care might enhance the process of becoming married. Chapter 6 examines the impact of our theologies *of* marriage on becoming married and then suggests a theology *for* marriage, or *marital habitus,* that might serve as a resource for planning the theme of a wedding.

Pre-Wedding Work:
A New Approach to Marriage Preparation

In the early decades of this century, the primary focus of premarital work was on the rite itself, the nature and meaning of Christian marriage, and the role of religion in the home.[2] The emphasis was on instruction. If people were not allowed to be married in a church, it was for ecclesiastical or theological reasons. The intent was to protect the institution of marriage itself. Even in Protestant churches that do not regard marriage as a sacrament, ministers were reluctant, on religious grounds, to marry divorced persons.

Over the last several decades, the emphasis of premarital counseling has shifted to the psychological compatibility of the couple. The aim has been to help couples see the areas of strength and vulnerability in their individual and collective histories. On some occasions, ministers have refused to conduct a wedding if there are signs of serious psychological incompatibility. A variety of testing instruments have been developed to help couples see themselves and their relationship as clearly as possible.³ Although these inventories may be used to predict marital success, their chief function is to initiate honest conversation between individuals planning to marry about matters of significance in their life together.

Couples remain cautious about revealing anything that might lead anyone to doubt the sincerity of their love or the viability of their relationship. They are, after all, in love. Nothing else matters. We have learned that talking about one's family of origin is more familiar and less scary and, therefore, more productive than examining a relationship still in the process of formation. *The pastoral pre-wedding task is to link the legacies from their families of origin with the values of the couple and the stories of the Christian tradition in order to understand more clearly their influence and to plan a wedding that symbolizes how they want to become married.* The couple are encouraged to understand their relationship in the light of the legacies that each brings to the process of forming a family.

Looking at Family from a Life-Cycle Perspective

Each of the five volumes in this series on Family Living in Pastoral Perspective will examine one of the changes that can be expected in the ordinary life cycle of a family. For every transition, there is frequently an event or events that initiate these five family tasks: leaving home, becoming married, raising children, promising again, and living alone. In this volume, the wedding is the event that initiates the task of becoming married. As a family moves through its history, the tasks accumulate and then eventually are reduced, as Figure 1 suggests. Like any schema, this figure does not fully represent actual living. There will be many variations, because people divorce and remarry, because some people leave home and then live alone, and because people marry but do not have children. For those people who marry and have children, however, these transitions and tasks mark out relatively predictable changes over time that define a family's history.

FIGURE 1
Transitions in the Family Life Cycle

Transitional Event	Leaving home events	Wedding	Birth of first child	Last child leaves	Death of a spouse
Family Tasks	Leaving home	Becoming married	Raising children	Promising again	Living alone
	Identity formation	Leaving home	Becoming married	Raising children	Identity re-formation
		Identity formation	Leaving home	Leaving home	
			Identity formation		

Families change because individual members change as they grow up and grow older. In that sense, the family is never a fixed sum. The needs of the family as a whole also change as a consequence of changes in membership and family circumstances. Individual transitions into and out of different family relationships and roles—such as leaving home, becoming married, becoming parents, coping with living alone—are interrelated with changes in the family as a system. Some of those changes are anticipated, some are not. The ability to adapt to change is therefore an essential characteristic of a family's capacity to move toward a future in which God is always making something new.

The particular, intimate, often conflicted human crucible that we call the family begins to shape us even before birth. Our families hand us a legacy—their sense of what is right and wrong, their rituals, their peculiar rules—all with the same sense that these are not peculiar at all, but the universal rules by which human beings live. It is often a shock to discover that our family's way is only one of many ways, and that the way we thought was universal might not even be the best way. The legacies we have received from our families of origin are the first and most powerful resource we have to negotiate the transitions and changes that mark our family's history.

The family as a social system changes according to its own history of evolving tasks. Each major transition in its life cycle offers a family the possibility of change. Such moments of transition create a crisis in the ordinary sense of that word because it is a turning point at which things will get either better or worse. It is not really possible to have change without crisis or without grief. A family's capacity to grieve its anticipated as well as its unanticipated losses will in large measure determine its ability to live through the crises of change. If marriage preparation ignores the changes and contradictions in becoming married that evoke grief and sadness, it will impede rather than enhance the possibility that God is doing a new thing in the forming of this new family.

This emphasis on the family's life cycle is the most practical and effective way of helping people understand the family as a social unit with a life and history of its own. It also provides a framework for thinking about how ordinary pastoral interventions related to the church's ritual life correspond to critical moments of transition in the family's history. The church's ministry with families often requires a delicate balance between attending to the needs of individuals in transition and responding to the needs of the family as a whole that is itself experiencing change.

The Paradox of Family Living

If change is central to the vitality of a family's life over time, paradox is what gives shape to its meaning and sustains its well-being in time. Paradox remains even when change occurs. We have to leave home in order to marry. Becoming married requires a balance between community and individual autonomy, between self-determination and sacrifice, between private and public realities, and between continuity and discontinuity with one's past. Families are likely to get in trouble when they do not keep alive both dimensions of a paradox. On the other hand, families remain vital if they can stay in the contradictions that finally only God can resolve. *The paradoxical reality of becoming and being married is the central theme of this book.*

For everyone who marries, it is necessary to decide in conversation with one's partner what to keep and what to discard of the legacy that each has received from his or her family of origin. This is one instance of the paradox of continuity and discontinuity in family living. If the loyalty to or preference for the values and traditions from one's family is strong, the new family being formed could look like a clone of the wife or husband's family of origin.

Maintaining continuity with one's family of origin is often a major source of conflict between husbands and wives early in

9

the process of becoming married. Competing preferences for daily rituals, conflicting values that shape how leisure time is spent, or different traditions about birthday celebrations may all become tests of loyalty. What begins as a small discussion about serving guests coffee with the meal or after the meal may become a cosmic conflict about which family is more sophisticated or cultured. Becoming married is a process that is forged in the crucible of the grief of letting go and the transforming promise of something new.

If paradox is at the center of any theology of the family, and essential for its spiritual vitality, then our ministry with families may in fact require that we intensify the creative tensions by "saying the other side." It is our pastoral task to intend paradox precisely because the contradictions in our lives that cannot be resolved often become the occasion for transformation. Paradox is not just a therapeutic tool or a means to effect some new resolution, but it can be an end in itself and a normal state. The helper's task is to assist people to live in the paradoxes of existence that are central to family well-being throughout the cycles of life.

Acknowledgments

This is the second book of a series on Family Living in Pastoral Perspective. The entire series is the outcome of years of collaboration with Kenneth R. Mitchell. Unfortunately, Ken died suddenly of a heart attack on February 18, 1991, before this project could be completed. Although this volume has been written with Cotton Fite, the spirit of Ken Mitchell is very much present. Cotton and I hope we have honored his memory by what we have written. I am grateful to the friends (new and old) who have agreed to join with me in completing this endeavor: *Raising Children*, with Susan B. W. Johnson; *Promising Again*, with David Hogue and Marie McCarthy, S.P.; and *Living Alone*, with Freda Gardner. The collaboration with each of these authors has enriched the project as a whole.

Over the years students, friends, clients, and participants in workshops have taught us about becoming married by telling their stories. The stories of some of them have been disguised in order to be included in this volume. While their real names do not appear, these people who have shared the joys and sorrows of becoming married have been internal conversation partners for us in writing this volume. The stories ascribed to Herbert or Cotton are, however, the stories of the authors.

There are specific people who must be thanked for their contributions to the volume. It is only possible to thank anonymously all the colleagues who have offered a suggestion or listened to a paragraph or ventured a critique that has shaped the development of this book. John Beck, JoAnn Post, Bradley Brauer, Paul S. Hammer, Linda Evans, and Doug Dowling offered very helpful suggestions from the perspective of pastoral ministry. John Callewaert, Joan Kellenweg, Catherine Boone, Thomas Kosnick, Gilbert Febos, Joy Anderson, Joel Anderson, Paulien Kleingeld, and Brigid Murphy-Racey read all or portions of the manuscript from the perspective of being *in* the process. Mary Huffman did very helpful research for chapter 4. Karen Speerstra continues to be a support for me about writing clearly and directly. And, last but not least, Harold Twiss—it has been a gift to us that he is a patient but persistent man as well as a wise editor.

Becoming married is a wonderful, exciting adventure and a painful, complicated process that usually takes longer than we think it should. Cotton and I hope that people who are becoming married and those who assist them in the process will find both illumination and encouragement in this volume.

HERBERT ANDERSON

Epiphany 1993

1

LEAVING COMES
BEFORE CLEAVING

THE PROCESS of becoming married has many beginnings. For some, it begins when people meet for the
first time or when at least one person in the relationship decides
that "this is the one for me." For others, it begins with the mutual declaration of love or the decision to live together or the private commitment to marry and the public announcement of that
intention. Yet others may identify the beginning of the process
with the wedding, when the couple declare publicly that from
now on they will be devoted to the task of becoming married.
After the wedding, even more aspects of the process unfold. Decisions that couples must make throughout—some small, some
large, some expected, some surprising—will continue the
process, but may, as in the instance of Tony and Jennifer, mark
the end of the relationship.

> Tony and I met in the lunchroom where we both work.
> Although I was just coming off a serious love affair, there
> was an immediate attraction, which was mutual. I liked
> his eyes. He liked my wit. And he was the most gentle
> man I had ever met. When two of my roommates moved
> out of our apartment quite suddenly, it seemed logical for
> Tony to move in with me. When my father asked what
> our living together meant, I said that Tony and I had a se-
> rious relationship. In my mind, it was not yet a permanent
> commitment. When Tony's mother asked me over pasta

when we planned to get married, I got nervous. Even though I knew I loved Tony, I was not sure that I wanted to be tied down by marriage quite yet. When the company offered Tony a wonderful promotion in Schenectady, New York, we had to decide something. He was very clear that he wanted us to get married and move to his new job. I was equally clear that I wanted to be married to Tony but I did not intend to leave my work or my friends and family in Chicago. Tony took the job.   (Jennifer)

Each moment in the process of becoming married requires commitment. Sometimes a commitment like deciding to live together, which is initially tentative or temporary, becomes permanent. Sometimes it does not. When Tony's mother asked about marriage, what had seemed to Jennifer to be a private and provisional arrangement suddenly had become a public relationship with expectations of permanence. Tony and Jennifer learned that making the kind of commitments that are part of becoming married can be very costly, sometimes too costly. Those commitments require intentionality, and almost always include experiences of loss that accompany letting go. We may fall in love or into marriage but we do not *fall* into becoming married. That requires self-conscious intent.

You Must Cleave Before You Can Cleave

There is an archaic word that has been used to refer to this process of committing to another person in marriage that has an appropriate double meaning. *To cleave* means to be attached or united closely in interest or affection, or to adhere with strong attachment. Cleaving is like clinging or sticking. In the King James Version of the biblical passage that most directly refers to the process of becoming married, cleaving comes after leaving. ("Therefore shall a man leave his father and his mother, and shall cleave unto his wife: and they shall be one flesh," Gen. 2:24.) In a literal sense, this sticking or adhering is what makes it possible to make one flesh out of two.

14

The word *cleave* also means to sever, to part or disunite, even if it must be done by force. It takes force to cleave a rock or a piece of wood. The implication of this usage is that cleaving is a separation of parts previously united. The same word carries both meanings of the process of becoming married: to cleave or separate oneself from one's origins in order to cleave or attach to someone in the bonds of marriage. In that sense, it is accurate to say that one must "cleave in order to cleave."

This link between separating from one's family of origin and attaching to someone to form a new family is the central theme of this book. *Leaving home is a necessary precondition for the process of becoming married.* Like leaving home, the process of becoming married takes time. It begins before the wedding but is not likely to be completed until much later, when both partners in a marriage discover and acknowledge that the emotional bond between them is deep and sure. The relationship between the wedding and these two interconnected movements of leaving home and becoming married looks something like Figure 2.

FIGURE 2

		W	
PRIMARY...........Leaving Home		E	.....Becoming Married
		D	
		D	
SECONDARY .....Becoming Married		I	.....Leaving Home
		N	
		G	

Although the bonding process undoubtedly begins early in the relationship, we believe that the primary work of the couple prior to the wedding is (1) to further the task of leaving home and understand the lingering impact of one's family of origin on the new family they are forming, and (2) to plan a wedding that appropriately ritualizes the twin movements in becoming married and anticipates the kind of family the couple would like to become. *The wedding ceremony is the transitional event that publicly inaugurates a new family task: becoming married.*

To Make One's Way by Leaving

It is necessary to leave home in order to become married. In the first book of this series, *Leaving Home,* this emotional life task was defined in the following way: *"Leaving home means a readiness, willingness, and ability to make one's own decisions, and to make one's way in the world without undue emotional dependence on the home one has come from."*[1] Leaving home is like cleaving in the sense of making one's way by "cutting or separating" from one's home of origin. Leaving home may or may not include a physical separation, but it must involve some emotional differentiation from our home of origin. Couples who are physically separated from their first families may cleave without leaving. Because they feel isolated, their marital bond may be strengthened even though the separation from home remains incomplete.

Leaving home takes time. It usually includes many events or moments in which the leaver makes a decision or takes an action that establishes a greater sense of autonomy in relation to the leaver's family of origin. Some of those events are marked by the physical departure of a son or daughter from the home of his or her origin; others revolve around an emotional separation that enables the departing child to claim his or her own sense of self. Deciding where one lives or works or what one studies at school or what one reads or thinks or believes or buys all may become pivotal moments in the process of leaving home. This process of leaving home is enhanced when parents are able to let their children go with a blessing.

For many centuries and in many cultures still today, children are not expected to leave home until they marry. The wedding is *the* watershed leaving-home event in those cultures. When that is the case, leaving-home issues are likely to dominate preparation for the wedding. Not all children are free to marry, however. In some cultures the role of caring for parents is determined by the birth order. In other instances, children choose or are chosen by the family to care for parents or a parent. Either way, the freedom to marry is limited by the responsibility of children to care for their parents.

In Western industrial societies, more often than not, children physically leave home before they marry.[2] This freedom to leave home but not marry is relatively recent in human history. When men and women marry later, it is likely they will live by themselves or with friends, often some distance from their home of origin, before marriage. That physical distance usually enhances the process of leaving home for adult sons and daughters. When that is the case, marriage preparations are likely to focus more on the bonding dimensions of becoming married than on the leaving.

There is no guarantee, however, that sons or daughters who have left home physically have effected the emotional separation that is necessary to make the kind of commitment to another person that becoming married demands. Consider this story.

> The full realization of leaving home began when I was married. I was an only child and very close to my parents. I had been in the pastoral ministry for eight years before I married. My wife likes to remind me that it was a very big change when I no longer sent my washing "home" to my mother to do. It was difficult for me to make room for my wife's things in the house where I had lived by myself for eight years. And I had long-established patterns of living that were not easy to change. But what I am most aware of is that home ties were severed with marriage. I could not depend on my mother in the same way again.
>
> (Charles)

What Charles discovered is that leaving home often takes more time and requires more effort than we think it should. We forget that the lengthy period of both physical and emotional dependence at the beginning of human life inevitably means that we are emotionally attached to the home of our origins. It is therefore understandable that the change in emotional allegiance that is necessary in order to become married will also take time. The process of shifting emotional loyalties does not happen overnight.

Even when the process goes well and leaving home has been done well, the first years of married life are likely to include some residue of the struggle for emotional separation from our first families. The process of leaving home continues after the wedding even though it now is, or at least should be, of secondary importance. Making a decision on how or where to spend birthdays or holidays often evokes conflict about loyalty for the spouse who comes from a "close-knit family." When the emotional roles that children have in a family, like entertaining parents or keeping the peace in a troubled marriage or rescuing mother from depression, have not been altered by the leaving-home process, a married son or daughter may choose for a parent rather than a spouse and the process of becoming married. *When leaving home has not sufficiently occurred prior to the wedding, the process of becoming married will take longer.* We will return to this theme in chapter 5 when we examine the process of becoming married after the wedding.

The focus of this chapter is on the time before the wedding, when leaving home is still a primary task. There are many significant moments in which choosing for the one we intend to marry challenges our sense of self, actualizes our freedom to decide, and thereby solidifies our autonomous agency. Commitments that are made in private become leaving-home moments when they are made public. How one chooses to make public the commitments that have been made privately may or may not help the emotional separation from our homes of origin. Figure 3 shows this movement between private and public action in order to illustrate how the process before the wedding continues to ritualize leaving home.

FIGURE 3

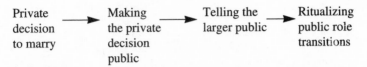

Private decision to marry → Making the private decision public → Telling the larger public → Ritualizing public role transitions

Leaving Home and the Decision to Marry

In those cultures in which the selection of a marital partner is a matter of free choice, that decision is determined by factors like mutual attractiveness and declarations of love. Studies in mate selection continue to confirm the significance of romantic love in the decision to marry.[3] There are other factors as well. Sons, it is said, will hope to marry someone like their mother in the hope of continuing to be taken care of or quite unlike their mother in order to be free of confining nurture. Daughters may also look for a replica of their fathers if their relationship with their father was dependable and supportive or someone quite different if the relationship to father was conflicted or abusive. Sometimes very pragmatic factors related to career plans or educational options weigh heavily in the decision to marry or the unexpressed expectations of marriage. While it is not the purpose of this book to examine in depth the selection of a mate, it is important to recognize that who and how one chooses to marry may be an act of separation from the home of one's origin that *may give the appearance of leaving home* but not effect emotional separation.

When the choice of a mate is in opposition to the advice or preference of parents, the wedding may become what the family therapist Murray Bowen once described as "an emotional cutoff," an act of separating that makes returning home difficult. Such a marriage succeeds only if it continues to be an act of rebellion against parental power. On other occasions, the choice of a partner has led to rejection by one's family even though that is not the son or daughter's intent. Marriages across cultures or races or socioeconomic class are the primary occasion for such radical action. For Mario, simply deciding to marry without parental consultation was enough to evoke the rage of his father.

> I am the third of eight children from a family of Filipino origins. I am the only one in my family to finish college on my own. One year after I finished college, I was a CPA with a good job in a bank and in love with Vickie. We decided to marry without consulting my parents. I knew I was violating the Filipino tradition. A man proposes to a woman, but it is his parents who "ask for her hand" from her parents. I was 27, and I thought I was old enough to make up my own mind. Besides, I was still angry that nobody had supported me through school the way others in my family had been supported financially. My parents liked Vickie, but they refused to come to the wedding not only because I violated my family's culture but because I bragged in anger about my independence from the family.   (Mario)

It is not always possible to predict the conflicts that will trigger a family's rejection of a child because of who or how they marry. In the story above, however, Mario anticipated his family's response and in fact may have triggered it. From a systemic perspective, conflicts between parents and children during the process of becoming married are seldom one-sided. More often than not, as in Mario's case, the conflict is related to unresolved leaving-home/letting-go agenda. A family life-cycle event turned sour and the task of becoming married was made more difficult because, at the same time that he announced his intent to marry Vickie, Mario chose to express angry feelings left over from the task of leaving home. When a transitional event like a wedding or the birth of the first child is contaminated by uncompleted prior tasks in the family's life cycle, the new life-cycle task will be more difficult to complete.

Deciding to live together may come before or after the public announcement of the engagement. Whenever it occurs, however, it is another decision that men and women make that may have as much to do with leaving home as with becoming married. We will discuss the consequences of living together for pre-wedding work in chapter 4. For this discussion, it is enough to note that if deciding to live together is a radical departure from the values of their first families, it may function as a leaving-home moment for one or both persons in the relationship even if that is not their conscious intention.

Making Public the Private Commitment to Marry

The announcement to one's family of origin of plans to marry is another pre-wedding moment that may also be a leaving-home event. Sons or daughters making this announcement hope that their families will like their choice of mate as much as they do. It may be a particularly anxious moment if the family is meeting the potential spouse and new member of the family for the first time. And if sons or daughters are only beginning their emotional separation from home, then announcing their intent to marry without parental endorsement becomes a highly charged moment. Both the autonomy of sons or daughters and the family's way of being are on the line. The complexity of mixing these agendas is one good reason why it is better to leave before you cleave.

The family's response to a child's intent to marry is also complex. It is a test of the family's hospitality and of its willingness to expand the boundaries of the system in order to make room for this stranger chosen by one of its own members. We can all tell stories of sons- or daughters-in-law who were never fully accepted into the family of their spouse. One of the most important tasks that a family must accomplish is to expand its circle in order to make room for the spouses of children. It is, as we will note in the concluding chapter, the willingness of a family to be hospitable that will enhance the prospect of welcoming into the family's sphere the stranger whom a son or daughter has chosen. When families are unable to extend this welcome, sons and daughters are put in an awkward position of choosing between spouse and family.

Children who consult with parents on the decision to marry this or that person are of course not obligated to follow the advice. Asking for advice is a way of including parents in the process. Parents who insist that they know what is best for their children—even more than the children themselves do—run the risk of excluding themselves. They may insist that their opinion prevail, and if it does not, they do not feel obligated to support a marriage they believe was ill-advised from the beginning. It is often the anticipation of parental opposition that prompts sons and daughters to elope or announce their marriage after the fact. Eloping in order to marry is similar to the pattern of *hidden departures* or "sneaky leaving" described in the previous volume in this series.[4]

John Hersey wrote a short story in which the oldest son, Gordon, returns home for Thanksgiving at age thirty-eight with his friend Beverly Zimmer. His brother Peter was there with his family. So were Uncle Solbert and Aunt Beth and assorted family friends. Thanksgiving dinners were the joy and victory of Gordon's puritan mother. This particular Thanksgiving dinner had been marked by lively and sometimes feisty conversation. Beverly had held her own. At one point, when the conversation seemed too hostile for Gordon, he proposed a toast to "the two women I love most in this world." Fortunately, Beverly spilled her wine so the substance of the toast was overlooked. When that crisis had been averted with a generous dose of salt, Gordon's mother turned to Beverly and said, "Tell me more about my Gordon."

"Well," Bev said, "he's sort of muh-muh . . . m-*my* Gordon right now."

"Ah," Mrs. Bronson said. "You stake a claim. Do you believe his intentions are honorable, as they used to say?"

"Better ask him," Beverly said, without a trace of a stammer.

"Gordon," his mother said, "serve some more turkey to whoever wants it, please."

Gordon felt a stab of anger. Having said that he and Peter had reverted to being eight and ten years old at her table, his mother was now, for her purposes, treating him like a child. Staking *her* claim, he guessed. Careful to control his voice, he said, "Beverly and I are going to be married."

Uncle Solbert tore his paper hat off and waved it in circles over his head and shouted, "Hurray!"

"Congratulations," Mr. Cannahan said to Beverly, looking heartbroken.

"My God," Peter said.

"And you chose to tell me this at Thanksgiving dinner?" Gordon's mother said.

"I thought you'd be happy for me, Mother."

"Oh, but I am," she said, her voice trembling. "You have picked a winner. You've shown very good sense, Son." She turned to Beverly and said, her eyes brimming, "I have liked you, Miss Zimmer, from the moment you walked in the front door. My Gordon, if you will permit me to call him that once more, is a very lucky boy."

After a long pause Beverly said, "Your p-peach ch-chutney is the b-best I ever tasted."

"Thank you, my dear." Gordon saw his mother's face relax into an awkward smile of surrender, and he felt a rush of contrition and pity. She was amazing.[5]

With minor variations here and there, this story is repeated again and again as sons and daughters announce their intent to marry. The response of families ranges from delight to disappointment to outright disapproval. Even when parents are happy about a son or daughter's choice of mate, it is still a time of sadness. Mrs. Bronson could no longer say "my Gordon" because he belonged to someone else. And Gordon had made a choice that his mother approved of, but without her help. That is a great loss for those parents who need their children to depend on them. Beverly actually broke the ice and forced Gordon's announcement of their upcoming marriage. Even so, it was a leaving-home moment for Gordon at age thirty-eight. If his mother had not approved of the choice, Gordon would have been faced with an even more difficult differentiating task: to disagree with his mother about his own life.

The dance between children and parents is delicate in those cultures in which sons and daughters are free to choose their own mates. Parents would like to be consulted, or at least believe that their opinion counted. When children live far from their home of origin, the evaluation of a child's choice often is made on the basis of first meetings that are already very strained. Mrs. Bronson's approval of Beverly was determined by her intuitions and first impressions. Children would like their parents' blessing on the choice of a mate without strings attached. When parents have specific expectations of the kind of person their child should marry, this delicate pre-wedding dance may become a struggle for freedom and autonomy.

In response to the practice of parents forcing their children into unwanted marriages, Luther wrote a treatise in 1524 entitled *That Parents Should Neither Compel Nor Hinder the Marriage of Their Children and Children Should Not Become Engaged Without the Consent of Their Parents.*[6] Luther believed that women and men were to find in marriage the things they naturally desire, such as sex and offspring, mutual trust, and a life together. To force people together or apart against their desire threatens the purpose of marriage. The historian Steven Ozment has observed that "in matters of marriage, as in matters of faith, the Reformation opposed bullying the heart and conscience."[7] When couples make public their private decision to marry, they are usually seeking support and not critical examination. The support that sons and daughters rightfully expect comes more readily, however, when parents have been informed and perhaps even consulted in the process.

Reordering Friendships

Just as it is necessary to reorder patterns and relationships with parents and family, it is also necessary to reorder relationships with friends as part of the process of becoming married. People in this society who live some distance from the home of their origin often form a network of friends who become like family. They are the stable base of support for daily living. Jennifer was reluctant to follow Tony to Schenectady in part because of the friends she would have to leave behind. Friends may also feel as abandoned as some families do when "one of the gang" chooses someone for a special relationship that will need to become more exclusive. In some instances, the emotional ties to friends are so intense that they are more difficult to alter than family bonds. When women and men intending to marry are unable to establish enough privacy from friends to work at bonding and the formation of their own identity as a couple, the process of becoming married will be complicated.

> I had been living alone for about eight years when I met Joshua. In the first years, I had one "best friend" with whom I shared almost everything. We ate dinner together three times a week, took walks, and studied together. When she got a boyfriend, all of that changed quite suddenly. I was still her best friend outside the "relationship," but now she had someone else with whom to share thoughts and experiences on a daily basis. Even though I found new friends or intensified old relationships, I still felt abandoned. And when those new friends would get intimate relationships, the same thing would happen again.

> When I fell in love with Joshua, it happened again. Only this time I was the cause. My friendships with single persons lost their intensity. I felt very bad about not being able to spend as much time with friends as I had before. I tried not to let my relationship with Joshua change my old friendships, but of course it did. Once I had a partner, I was glad to be able to recover old friends who were married or had a special relationship.   (Roseline)

Becoming married does not mean the end of friendships. In fact, couples who are working at becoming married need as much support as they can muster for that task. It is necessary, however, to renegotiate the bonds with friends before the wedding so that it is clear to everyone that becoming married will be the primary agenda for the couple. Sometimes it is enough to spend less time with friends. In other circumstances, it is necessary to modify emotional involvements outside the marriage in order to make time and energy available for the task of becoming married. This commitment to reorder friendships for the sake of a marriage is complicated by a paradox that is at the center of marriage today: the commitment to be with another for better or worse should limit but not eliminate freedom for self-determination. We will return to this theme at a number of points in the volume because it is so critical for couples marrying today.

The *individualism* that has been characterized as common in American culture supports the idea that commitments like marriage make sense only when they further one's personal self-realization. Having friends is not as confining as being married. The process of becoming married is therefore complicated by our determination to think for ourselves, judge for ourselves, make our own decisions, live our own lives. True love, from this perspective, can occur only between autonomous individuals and, as Robert Bellah points out, "the only real social bonds are those based on the free choices of authentic selves."[8]

The central danger of radical individualism is that it seems to support only those commitments to others that are based on personal interest. The idea of marriage as a lifelong commitment does not fit easily with this emphasis on the individual as an unburdened self. For the survival of marriages and societies alike, we need to keep a balance between respecting the needs of the individual and considering the needs of the community. The struggle between the need to strengthen the social bonds of marriage and the importance of supporting freedom for self-determination in order to actualize one's gifts is another instance of the paradox of separateness and togetherness that we regard as central for effective family living.

Having friends who are like family also makes reordering friendship part of the process of becoming married. Leaving friends in order to marry has greater significance when the boundaries between family and not-family are fluid. The *floating family* is one term used to describe this way in which the affectional ties of a person are extended beyond the physical and relational ties that once defined the family. "The most important relationship in a person's life may be with a non-relative he or she virtually never sees, someone living thousands of miles away—an intense bond maintained entirely by electronic impulses, occasional visits and active imaginations."[9] The variety of technologies of communication make it possible to spend as much time being connected to friends far away as to those near at hand. The supportive friends that a couple make as a couple are also part of this reordering process.

It is unclear what form marriages and families will take in the decades ahead. One thing seems certain, however. The networks that people will identify as family are likely to be formed as much by choice as by bloodline. The German sociologist Ulrich Beck has observed that "each person's biography is removed from given determinations and placed in his or her own hand, open and dependent on decisions."[10] The same will be true for family living. For that reason alone, making choices about renegotiating friendships will be an essential part of the process of becoming married.

For This Reason Shall a Man
Leave Father and Mother

Our discussion of the process of leaving home as a necessary prerequisite to forming a marital bond is consistent with the intent of the biblical mandate first recorded in the book of Genesis and reiterated by Jesus. "Therefore a man leaves his father and his mother and clings to his wife, and they become one flesh" (Gen. 2:24). When this passage is repeated by Jesus, the notion of one flesh is reinforced. "So they are no longer two, but one flesh. Therefore what God has joined together, let no one separate" (Mark 10:8b–9). This admonition to leave father and mother, which originally was a geographic necessity because the new couple had to live in the context of one extended family, is even more crucial when we understand becoming married as an intellectual and emotional process. For the modern marriage, the union is more about emotional bonds than about geographic location. And leaving father and mother in order to become married is more a matter of shifting loyalties than of place of residence.

Love Is Risky

The biblical reference to leaving and cleaving is a summary of the creation of humankind according to the Yahwist writer. What was originally one flesh (Adam) and becomes two (woman and man) longs to be one flesh again. It is as if the biblical writer is attempting to explain this love that is "strong as death, / passion fierce as the grave" (Song of Solomon 8:6). Because clinging or cleaving between woman and man is so central to human living, people are even willing to set aside the secure love of parents in order to be as they once were: one flesh. Despite the original longing to be one with another human being, the love of a woman and a man is risky. It is not surprising that people want to hold on to the security or dependability of parental love. Our emphasis on leaving father and mother is a recognition that most marriages today are such a complex process that any withholding of emotional investment is likely to impede the desired union of two people.

The insistence that it is the man and not the woman who must leave father and mother is a curious thing, given the patrilineal character of Hebrew culture. It may be, as von Rad has observed, that this statement preserves "something of a time of matriarchal culture."[11] What we understand as an emotional process today was originally a practical geographic action. The couple needed to be located in one larger, extended-family system. Ordinarily one would expect that the woman must leave her father and mother in order to join her husband's extended family. But even in a patriarchal society, a man can join the family of his wife.

The interpretation of Genesis 2:24 throughout the church's history has changed, but it has almost always fostered a negative view of women. In the second century, for example, Philo suggested that a woman should not have to leave her parents to be joined to her husband because the strength or audacity of the man is more bold. By contrast, Chrysostom, one of the early church fathers, described the process of becoming married as we understand it, but he limited the leaving-home action to the woman. It is altogether impossible, he suggested, that the bride be united to a husband unless she has forgotten her parents and those who reared her, and unless she has given over her will, whole and entire, to him who will be joined to her as her bridegroom.[12] What is necessary to become married has always been the same: leaving father and mother. What has changed throughout the centuries is the one who does the leaving. We understand ourselves to be in the spirit of that tradition when we insist that women and men alike must leave father and mother in order to cleave to their husband or wife—and become one flesh.

Becoming One Flesh

The way in which scripture describes the bond of marriage as "one flesh" has also been interpreted in a variety of ways. It may mean offspring—that a union between a man and a woman is not complete until it becomes one flesh in a child. It may mean the sexual consummation that occurs in intercourse. Or it may be understood as the creation of a small society in which two people are related to each other across the full spectrum of possibilities for human relationships. The metaphor of one flesh is not just about what our sexual relations ought to be, but what we hope they will be like. Our sense of duty is joined with our desire, our longing for an intimacy that gives life.

"One flesh" is a useful metaphor because it reminds us of the embodied character of the marriage union we seek. Bonding is not simply a spiritual matter; it is about flesh and bones. And however women and men are different, they are formed of the same substance. Old Testament theologian Dianne Bergant has observed that these words in Genesis 2:23a have psychological as well as physiological meaning. The first implies power and the second weakness. "This is 'bone of my bones,' or strength of my strengths, 'and flesh of my flesh,' or weakness of my weaknesses, and everything in between. The man recognizes that the woman is the one with whom he can interact totally. He is no longer alone. He now has a suitable partner."[13] Understood in this way, the metaphor of "one flesh" is more about what women and men have in common rather than about unity of being or the merger of personalities.

We will return to the images of marriage in the concluding chapter of this book. We mention the metaphor "one flesh" at this point only because the church has tended to emphasize the oneness or unity aspect of marriage to the exclusion of autonomy or separateness. This emphasis on union or "one flesh" has been symbolized in wedding ceremonies by the bride and the groom blowing out their separate candles after lighting the wedding candle. Our approach to the wedding presupposes that marriage is a complicated and ever-changing balance of separateness and togetherness. The "one flesh" of marriage is always composed of two distinct bodies. The biblical text needs to be expanded to acknowledge the reality that when two people who have both left father and mother become one flesh, they remain two distinct bodies with two distinct identities.

A Home with a Room of One's Own

The image of marriage as "one flesh with two distinct bodies" is another expression of the main theme of this book. *The paradox of leaving and cleaving presumes a particular understanding of family living in which separateness and togetherness are kept in delicate balance.* Leaving in order to cleave presumes the formation of a new family in which individual uniqueness is honored and encouraged, in which clear boundaries make for solid bonds, in which community and autonomy are both valued, and in which everyone has "a room of one's own."

— A home with a room of one's own is a family in which it is possible to risk being separate because there is enough caring to keep people together.

— A home with a room of one's own is a place where clear but permeable boundaries make intimacy possible by protecting individual differences while encouraging interaction.

— A home with a room of one's own is where there is time to be alone and time to be with others and freedom to choose when to be alone and when to be with others.

— A home with a room of one's own fosters empathy and the recognition that the other's experience is as valid as our own.

The image of "a home with a room of one's own" emphasizes that commitment to community in family does not diminish the importance of individual uniqueness and autonomy. A "room of one's own" may be a special chair for reading or the workbench in the basement to which one can go to be alone, or it may simply be the ongoing awareness that even though a family is close, it still honors each individual's thoughts, feelings, wishes, and fantasies as unique and sacred.

It is not easy to establish a personal space or "room" in the home even with support, as seen in Ted and Connie's experience:

When Ted and I were first married, we lived with his parents because we had one semester of school left. They were great. His mom helped us out by making breakfasts and doing our laundry. Ted's family was one of the things that attracted me to him. They seemed so close and attentive to each other. In contrast to my family, which majored in confusion and chaos, Ted's home was a peaceable haven. Even though his family was not always open to those outside, they had made me feel very welcome. After we lived there awhile, I began to feel confined. I found more and more excuses to study at the library just to get away from the hovering interest of Ted and his mother.

After we graduated, Ted and I found a one-bedroom apartment near the school where we both taught. The apartment had to have a living room big enough for the large oak desk Ted had inherited from his grandfather. For Ted, the desk was a symbol of our togetherness. When Ted wanted us to read quietly together in the same room, I wondered what he was keeping from me. I preferred to work alone. So I claimed the bedroom as my space because it seemed to me that the living room belonged to Ted and his oak desk. When Ted left his socks and dirty underwear on the bedroom floor, it felt to me like a violation of my space. I grew up in a home with eight children, three bedrooms, and no privacy. It seems to me that most of our fights in the first two years were about my need for a life of my own.

We had three children in a hurry. While they were small I did not work outside the home. When our youngest child was old enough for nursery school, I enrolled in law school. It had been a lifelong dream to be a lawyer. Ted was not too eager, but finally agreed when his mother volunteered for late afternoon child care twice a week. It was a great time for me and a hard time for Ted. I discovered creative energies and intellectual gifts that strengthened my sense of autonomy. I had only a card table in our bedroom to work on but I did not really care. My thoughts and ideas were my own. I think Ted was attracted to my new independent energy and frightened by it. His understanding of being a family was still the cocoon that his mother created, in which it seemed to me that people were so close that they could breathe in unison.   (Connie)

Ted and Connie each embodies one half of the paradox that is central for effective family living. Ted's family majored in togetherness. Their warmth was real and their home was a safe haven closed off from the world. But inside the family there was so much closeness that it was not surprising that Ted was both frightened by and attracted to the fierce independence of Connie and her family. Becoming married is a delicate process of finding a balance between uninterrupted togetherness and exaggerated separateness. The aim is a marital bond with clear but permeable boundaries. A home with a room of one's own is a metaphor that points to the separate/together paradox that is essential for becoming married.

It is easier to declare this paradox than it is to accomplish it, however. As we have already noted, there are powerful cultural factors that promote autonomy and economic mobility and freedom for self-determination at the expense of time enough together to become married. The process of bonding is also hindered when husbands and/or wives are too close to their parents and do not know it. Hidden loyalties and excessive dependence on one's family of origin impede forming a new family. This paradox between being separate and being together is inevitable if one holds the belief that enduring love occurs between autonomous individuals. One of the ironies of our time is that marriages are breaking up more frequently just as personal autonomy is enhancing this potential for real intimacy.

Conclusion

Our consideration of wedding preparation in the next three chapters builds on two principles that are both biblically true and psychologically valid. (1) *You must leave before you can cleave.* The process of becoming married includes separating from one's home of origin and joining or bonding with one's wife or husband. Prior to the wedding, the focus is primarily on continuing the leaving-home process, identifying one's family legacy, and noting the possible impact from one's family of origin on the new family that is being formed. Pastoral work with couples follows the same pattern. (2) *The image of one flesh needs to be expanded to include both aspects of the separate/together paradox which is fundamental for vital family living.* "A home with a room of one's own" is a metaphor that embodies this image of marriage as a balance between separateness and togetherness, between autonomy and community. The process of bonding following the wedding needs to keep alive this image of marriage.

We have identified a number of psychological and practical reasons why leaving must come before cleaving. The freedom to make an emotional commitment to another human being and to accept that person's claim on one's life depends on letting go of and being released from or at least redefining the claims and commitments of our families of origin and our friends. The longer it takes to effect an emotional separation from our family and friends, the longer it will take to become married. That process will include making all kinds of little decisions like how you sleep and when you eat or where you get undressed or how you read the morning paper or when you pray. The decision to leave home, however, is still primary. It is no wonder that becoming married is hard work that takes time, delicate negotiating, and a lot of goodwill.

2
A WEDDING OF STORIES

BECOMING MARRIED is a wedding of many stories. It
is a continuation of the particular story that began
when the couple first met. Because many people live away from
the home of their origin before they marry, each individual also
has his or her own unique narrative to fold into the common
story that is being formed. Those who have been married before
will have memories of a relationship that did not endure to include in the new story that is being written. Finally, there is the
legacy from each family of origin that is a major factor in forming a new family story.[1]

The Stories Families Tell

The legacy from our families of origin is kept alive by many
kinds of stories. They are the foundation for our future. Most of
the stories families tell are about ordinary events like holidays or
birthdays or vacations or dinners that come to have special meaning in their remembrance. We tell stories about the birth of a long-
hoped-for child or the death of a significant family member.

> I was the only child born to my parents after several years
> of marriage. My mother had an extremely difficult labor
> and an even more difficult time giving birth to me. I was
> in critical condition with a variety of injuries from the

complications of the delivery. So was my mother. I was baptized shortly after birth. After three days, both of us had made enough progress that we were taken off the critical list. It was then that I was named "Victor" by my father. This story is regularly told on my birthday. I am grateful to be alive. At the same time, I am reminded again and again how much it cost my mother to give me life. Sometimes I wish we could forget the story. (Victor)

The power of family stories to shape our attitudes and reinforce our obligations is illustrated by Victor's remembrance. The stories we tell are modified over time as the pain or the shame recedes. For Victor's mother, however, the pain of his birth was still vivid on his fortieth birthday. So was his sense of debt to her. In rehearsing this story in preparation for his second marriage, Victor finally determined that he needed to tell of his birth in a new way in order to be free to marry.

Some family stories are about unique personalities like Aunt Minnie, who ran a boarding house in the Depression, or José, who crossed the Mexican border illegally four times, or about Great-Aunt Agnes, who once modeled camisoles and ladies' undergarments. The members of Erma Johnson's family often recall how their ancestors survived slavery. The fact that Great-Uncle Bert owned the first automobile in Edison County is a matter of great pride whenever the Dennisons tell family stories. Stories like these that have been handed down from generation to generation often assume the status of legend. Whether family stories are true or not is not as significant as the meaning they have for the family's self-understanding.[2]

When families do not tell stories, it may be because they are very private or because communication is not a dominant part of their portfolio. However, some families do not tell stories because there are secrets to be kept. The secret may be about a grief that was too great to bear or so shameful that it must remain hidden. Even though such secrets may be several generations old, they continue to be a negative influence on a family's interaction in the present. Secret-keeping patterns diminish continuity and limit the kind of intimacy that story-telling creates. If those assigned the role of preserving the secrets are skilled at their task, others in the family may not even know that there are stories to be told. All they know is that their family does not tell stories or talk about itself.

> My great-great-grandfather was a Baptist minister who was a strong advocate for the cause of the North during the Civil War. Beyond making political speeches and preaching in that cause, he contributed his time as a volunteer chaplain in the South. While in the service of that military cause, he contracted dysentery, and became so sick that no one expected him to live. He was, however, sent back home by boat, and his wife nursed him back to health against all odds. He lived more than forty years after that. It was not until I read the diaries of his daughter that I learned that my sainted great-great-grandfather had been a morphine addict for those forty years.   (Jean)

In order for Jean's family to preserve the mythic character of the great-great-grandfather and the story of his heroic deeds, his vulnerability had remained a secret. It was not altogether surprising that Jean discovered several other secrets in the attic when the home that had been in the family for five generations was finally sold. Once she made the discovery about her great-great-grandfather, Jean also understood more clearly why her family never told stories. She also knew better why being vulnerable was so difficult for her.[3]

Families tell stories in order to maintain their foundational beliefs, sustain their unique identity, and reaffirm their common values. Even when we come from families that do not tell stories, every family has a history that is itself a narrative that will reveal its beliefs and values. When two people marry, they embark on a new story that incorporates the narratives from their past. Knowing and telling our family stories is a way of claiming our particular legacy. It is also a way of bonding, because marriage is a wedding of stories.

If becoming married is a wedding of stories, then prepara-tion for marriage must be an invitation to storytelling. If one's family of origin has a history of storytelling, it is relatively easy to engage the bride or groom in identifying the legacy that he or she brings to this wedding of stories. When there is resistance to storytelling for whatever reason, then it is more difficult—*and more important*—to help the bride or groom recover the stories of the family. Telling family stories is a critical part of the process of becoming married because it is a way for the couple to weave together their new story while at the same time pre-serving the thread of each separate narrative.

A Wedding Is More Parable Than Myth

For the Christian, understanding life in a narrative way moves beyond individual family stories or even societal sagas to the story of Jesus and the legacies of faith. Our identity as be-lievers is formed and sustained by telling stories about the human struggle to understand God's faithfulness. The story of Jesus is pivotal because it embodies the contradiction that is central for Christian living—life is found in losing it. For Chris-tians becoming married, the common task of making a new nar-rative out of the wedding of many stories is modified by the parabolic story of Jesus.

There are many ways to tell stories. The New Testament scholar John Dominic Crossan has identified myth and parable as two contrasting types of storytelling.[4] Myth, Crossan sug-gests, attempts to mediate between "irreducible opposites." The assumption is that reconciliation is always possible. Myth has a double function: it resolves what is contradictory and, perhaps more significantly, it creates a belief in the permanent possibility of reconciliation.

Parable is the opposite of myth. It is not a story that at-tempts to reconcile what is contradictory; rather, it actually cre-ates contradiction and the necessity of paradox. Unlike myth, which implies stability, parables are agents of change. It is para-ble that most clearly represents the life and ministry of Jesus.

A parable is a way of thinking about experience that rejects easy reconciliation. Thinking in parables has the potential to embrace both contradiction and death. For the Christian, the cross is the ultimate contradiction. Easter is possible only if we can embrace the cross event. For that reason, the death of Jesus is *the* parable at the heart of every narrative taken up in his name. Parable is paradox formed into story.

The wedding of Christians is like a parable because it too is governed by the fundamental principle that new life begins with loss. Though we may think of marriage only in terms of new life, this new life is not possible without innumerable losses. When we marry we are no longer "Daddy's girl" or "Mommy's boy" but an interdependent partner. In order to be a spouse, we will also need to turn our back on some past relationships and dreams. Despite our efforts to plan weddings of mythic proportions, the parabolic nature of marriage is inevitable.

If we understand the wedding of stories as parable, it will mean the death of old claims and old loyalties for the sake of something new that God is doing. Many of those claims and loyalties are embedded in the hidden expectations and secret alliances in our families of origin. Although one would hope that the process of leaving home which alters those claims has begun long before the wedding, we often need to rehearse our separation from home once again. Other claims today come from commitments to friends or careers that were made before we married. Letting go of familiar roles, dependable alliances, or cherished freedom is a profound loss. Ultimately, it means letting go of the myth that everything can stay the same and accepting the inevitability of change. It is for that reason that a wedding of stories is an experience of loss and grief.

The Wedding Ritual Includes Joy and Sadness

The new life of a marriage begins in the midst of many endings. The joy of bonding is balanced by the sadness of letting go of people and places and things and patterns of living that must change in order to become married. No wedding garment, seven-tiered wedding cake, string quartet, or sleek limousine can ultimately distract from the inevitability of loss. Because the wedding is a time of loss as well as adventure, it is a ritual of both sadness and joy. If we insist on a mythic beginning to marriage and ignore the parabolic dimension of the process, we will impede the possibility of change which is the source of all new life.

My mother died when I was nine. She developed a rare heart condition immediately after my brother was born. It was difficult for my father when she died. He was not prepared to be the only parent of four children from age fourteen to five months. Fortunately for all of us, my Italian grandmother took over.

About a year after Mother's death, my dad met a young widow who had two sons. When they married, they determined not to speak of their first spouses who had died and not to display any pictures of them. As a result, I grew up without any pictures and with *very* few memories of my mother. My stepmother was good to me, but throughout my adolescence I wished to know more about my birth mother. Whenever I asked my father about her, he would get a pained look and change the subject. Eventually I learned not to ask. Until I decided to get married.

The pastor who presided at our wedding kept asking me to ask my father about my mother. My father's response was the same as it had been, except once when he showed me a picture of my mother when they were married. At the rehearsal, I overheard the pastor observing to my father that it would be difficult to go through the wedding of his only daughter without thinking about her mother. My father shrugged it off and simply said what he had been saying to me—how happy he was that I was marrying such a nice man. We had the reception at my father's country club. When the master of ceremonies announced that the bride would dance the first dance with her father, he was nowhere to be found. He showed up an hour later

and told me he had talked to the pastor about my mother's
death for the first time in fifteen years.   (Veronica)

Veronica's story is a dramatic illustration of a common reality at weddings. Her father had been determined to participate
in his only daughter's wedding without thinking about her
mother, his first wife. A splendid wedding and a grand reception at his favorite country club could not, however, cover over
all the grief. He was not free to celebrate his daughter's marriage until he had mourned once again the death of her mother.
His efforts to keep the grief for the death of his first wife buried
had been counterproductive for relationships in the family, up to
and including the wedding of his only daughter.[5]
  The sadness of Veronica's father was appropriate for the
occasion. His inability to acknowledge that sadness was not. It
is unfortunate that wonderful moments like dancing the first
dance with your daughter are missed in order to keep grief hidden. Unfortunately, the breakthrough that occurred on the wedding night did not open up to new freedom for Veronica and her
brothers to talk about their mother. Several years later, a major
conflict erupted in the family when one of Veronica's brothers
chose to name his first daughter after his birth mother and not
his stepmother. We will consider the implications of the presence of grief for pre-wedding work again in chapter 4. It is our
hope that understanding the wedding ceremony as a parabolic
event will make it easier to recognize the unavoidable reality of
loss and grief, even at a time so full of joy.
  Despite (or perhaps because of) the sobering picture of marriage that is reflected in current divorce statistics, there is still a
strong impulse from culture and commerce and brides young and
old to plan dreamlike weddings. Personal blemishes and family
flaws and ordinary human imperfections like crying babies are
frequently hidden behind an elaborate and costly facade in order
to create a mythic beginning for a marriage. Families often
exhaust their savings in order to give a daughter the wedding
she has dreamed about since she began reading bride magazines

when she was ten. We are not against grand celebrations. If the family has the money to spend for a lavish wedding, it may not be good stewardship, but it is harmless enough for the couple to be king and queen for a day. We are more aware of the destructive power of inauthenticity and secret-keeping in family living. *A mythic wedding is not a good beginning, simply because marriage will inevitably be more like a parable. Family living is full of contradiction.*

This emphasis on parable as the metaphor for understanding the wedding is supported by two principles that are constant throughout this series. First, *paradox is a central characteristic of family living.* Becoming married is a process that includes two seemingly contradictory actions: leaving and cleaving. It should not be surprising, therefore, that the wedding is a moment of contradictory emotions: sadness and joy. Couples and families who ignore one half of the paradox or the other inhibit the process of becoming married. Second, *most families are good enough* to provide a context in which people grow to maturity. A mythic picture of the family is a denial of the limits of human creatureliness. And secret-keeping that denies imperfection or ordinary human vulnerability is a form of idolatry.

The Purpose of Family Storytelling

This emphasis on the inevitability of loss and grief is linked to one of our aims for pastoral work before the wedding: to enhance leaving for the sake of cleaving. The experiences of leaving home and letting go are themselves occasions for ordinary grieving. In the previous chapter, we examined actions prior to the wedding by which a private bond became a public commitment. Many of those moments enhanced the process of leaving home because they tested new loyalties and effected new status in the family system. *The first purpose of pastoral work with couples before the wedding is to encourage new and sometimes highly charged efforts to effect emotional separation from the home of one's origin.* Those who help couples prepare for a wedding are empathic advocates on behalf of sons and daughters leaving home so they can become married, while at the same time providing support for parents who are having a difficult time letting go.[6]

A wedding of stories is more than the private union of two people in love; it is inevitably a merger of families, which on occasion resembles "corporate takeover" of one family by another. Each of us brings to marriage a legacy of values and role expectations and patterns of interacting that we have received from our first family. For good or ill, our attitudes about marriage are unavoidably shaped by the families that first taught us what it means to be married. Some people who are preparing to marry have their family legacy and its lingering influence clearly in view. Most people do not. Most of us are influenced by assumptions about marriage and family traditions and stories that are not in our awareness.

The second task of pre-wedding work is to help each individual see clearly the family legacy and his or her role in it. Our intent is to foster curiosity about the family that was the context for each individual's development. People who struggle to survive in poverty or who are totally engrossed in the daily grind of living one step ahead of the bill collector may regard this focus on family legacy as an irrelevant luxury. Others who are too frightened to be curious may regard such exploration as risky. In such situations, telling a fictitious story about becoming married may help the couple reflect on their own experience.

We have found most couples planning to marry willing to tell family stories. That is especially true if we can make clear that the aim is understanding rather than evaluation. Telling our family's story is a way of identifying its claim on our lives. Sometimes simply telling the story to someone outside the family is itself an act of liberation from the constraints of a possessive family of origin. For example, Myleta became more aware during preparation for her wedding of the claim that her family had on her life. And then she understood what her grandmother had been saying to her for weeks before the wedding: "You are carrying too much to pick up the ruby." Storytelling may be a way of helping us understand when we are "carrying too much" and what we might need to leave behind in order to be free enough to cleave.

This agenda for pre-wedding work is no less important for people who have emotionally and physically left home and lived on their own before becoming married. Sometimes they have forgotten the influences from their home of origin. Others may believe that how they live is their own creation, until they discover after the wedding how much they are doing things just the way their parents did. It is difficult to ignore the image of marriage we have all internalized from our first families. Understanding the lingering impact from our homes of origin is therefore a significant agenda even for sons and daughters who have left home long before the wedding.

The third aim of pre-wedding work is to help the couple see more clearly their relationship to each other in the light of their relationships to their families of origin. This aim is often the by-product of telling family stories. Couples will begin to recognize how and in what ways their families have already shaped their relationship. They will discover significant parallels on their own initiative. What is important about this aim of pre-wedding work is that it helps the couple to be intentional about two questions: (1) What is there about your family of origin that you want to be sure to include in the new family you are forming? (2) What is there about your family of origin that you would not like to continue in your new family? What couples discover in exploring these questions is the need for and the difficulty of changing our loyalties.

People planning to marry are often surprised by a kind of love they have never known before. They may understand that the goodness of God's love is revealed in that love which motivates people to marry. Whenever two people marry, God is doing something new. We may not see it. We may even try to impede it. Yet most couples want their marriage to be something new and special even if they do not know how to make that possible. Something new is more likely to happen if we can increase our awareness of the legacy we bring to becoming married.

The Genogram as a Tool for Storytelling

Unless we come from a family of storytellers, we will need some assistance in thinking about family stories. The genogram is a very effective tool to facilitate telling stories for the sake of understanding one's family of origin. It is like a family tree, only more so. What makes a genogram different from a family tree is the stress on stories and traditions and emotional connections that go beyond mere facts. In a sense, the genogram is simply a vehicle for storytelling. There are insights that can be gained, however, just by putting on paper a picture of the family within.[7]

Like a family tree, a genogram seeks to identify two or three generations of membership in our first family. Unlike a family tree, stories and patterns of interacting and alliances are more important than the actual dates or places of birth. It does not matter whether one begins with the oldest or the youngest generation; the goal is to draw a map of the significant relationships of each family of origin from a multigenerational point of view. If you have a few models to start with, it does not take long to develop a distinctive approach to doing a genogram. Without the complications that are increasingly a part of family history today, the skeleton of a genogram will look something like Figure 4.

FIGURE 4
A Genogram

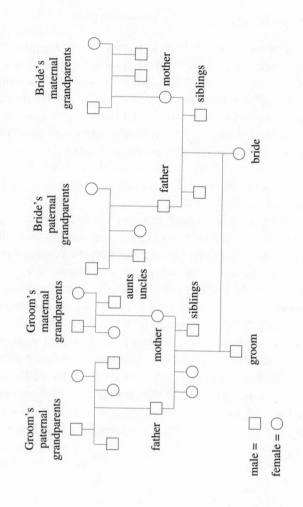

Groom's paternal grandparents

Groom's maternal grandparents

Bride's paternal grandparents

Bride's maternal grandparents

aunts uncles

father

mother

mother

father

siblings

siblings

groom

bride

male = □

female = ○

Because one of the goals of pre-wedding work is to clarify each individual's relationship to his or her first family, no story is unimportant in the creation of a genogram. Nor is any relationship insignificant. We are interested in the alliances that transcend generations and the impact of major family events over time. It need not be a problem that an individual does not know all the facts about births and deaths. Sometimes what we do not know reveals as much as what we do know. It is useful to do the genogram before going in search of information, because it helps to focus on the questions that need to be asked.

When the families we come from have not functioned well, there will be a reluctance to tell stories of things for which we are ashamed or to talk about relationships that are hurtful. Obviously, individuals should not be forced to tell stories they do not want to tell or talk about pain or shame they want to hide. There is usually more than enough material to explore in a family's history without such stories. Honoring their reluctance should, however, be linked with a recommendation to the couple that they share with one another what they cannot talk about in the presence of an outsider. It is also important to alert them to the possibility that they may attempt to create an impossibly ideal family in order not to be *at all* like the destructive families from which they came.

Telling the stories and exposing the family secrets enable a couple to confront the emotional power of their first families in order to intend something new. The process of telling and hearing each one's story in the context of a genogram enables a couple to think about their pasts and their future in a way that is nonthreatening and often pleasurable. It is one action that has the potential to effect both leaving and cleaving. Doing a genogram is a leaving-home event because it can enable an individual to gain more emotional distance by externalizing the picture of the family she or he carries within. It is a time of cleaving because partners regularly discover something more about the one they intend to marry or a commonality between them that strengthens their emotional bond.

The Advantages of a Genogram

If the relationship is the primary focus of premarital counseling, then psychological inventories or questionnaires are the useful tool for locating areas in the relationship in need of further exploration. Because we regard the invitation to storytelling to be an essential dimension of preparation for marriage, the genogram is the preferred method. It has other advantages, which are particularly beneficial in areas where pastoral ministry moves across cultures or among the poor or in areas of the world not yet technologized.

1. It does not presume literacy or even an extensive ability in the language being used. It is possible to do a genogram with someone with very limited language skills. It simply takes longer.

2. A genogram is portable and adaptable to a variety of situations. Ordinarily it is done on paper large enough to include all the various connections of people we call family. There are computerized versions of a genogram that can be used individually. It may be done on a blackboard, although that medium does not leave a permanent record that can be used at another time. A genogram may also be done on the sand in settings where there is neither paper nor blackboard. It is a method, unlike computerized questionnaires, that has maximum flexibility.

3. It diminishes defensiveness. When couples are in love or in heat or both, they are not generally open to exploring their relationship—out of fear that someone might tell them they should not get married. Even if couples are told that psychological inventories will not be used in that gatekeeping way, they are still cautious. The focus on family of origin that we are proposing defuses this worry. Moreover, talking about our families is something that is ordinarily done over coffee with friends or with perfect strangers at social gatherings.

4. The genogram builds a bond between the pastor and the couple. It is a common activity that becomes a part of the history they share together and, when appropriate, may be introduced at some point in the rituals that follow. It also provides a reference point for pastoral conversations after the wedding.

5. When it is not possible for one person of the marital couple to be present until just before the wedding, doing a genogram is still useful. Being clearer about legacy and continuing the process of leaving home are both individual tasks that can be worked on even if the couple are apart. Beginning to understand how or in what ways one's family of origin will influence becoming married may be done individually before it is done as a couple.

6. The genogram is a public document. Presumably the material discussed is generally known in the family. The primary focus is not on a relationship that is still quite private and is certainly still being formed.

7. Related to the public nature of the genogram, the focus on family of origin has the potential for making the wedding a many-generational event. People anticipating marriage should be encouraged to share what is produced with their parents, in the interest of initiating more conversation about the legacies of their history. One of the great advantages of the genogram in this regard is to give permission for people to ask questions about their families that they might not otherwise feel free to ask and bring to light previously hidden stories.

8. Doing a genogram can be fun.

Doing a Genogram

A variety of materials may be used to draw the genogram. A large art tablet or newsprint will do. The computerized forms that have been developed may make the process go more easily and neatly. Most families, however, are not neat. There is some advantage to creating a genogram that looks a little like the family itself. It is also important that the uniqueness of each family be preserved in the genogram. Different-colored pens or markers may help to highlight the differences between the various lines in the family's history. Ideally, the genogram will be done in such a way that the couple will be able to use it to foster further discussion prior to the wedding and in the first years of marriage. (See Appendix A for a description of symbols to use in sketching a genogram.)

Couples need not prepare for the genogram. Some people may be inclined to find out information on dates of birth or death that they would be embarrassed not to know. It is not necessary, however, to do extensive prior research. What we do not know about our origins is often as significant as what we do know. Moreover, the questions asked of the couple are likely to send them in a direction they might not have thought to pursue on their own. They are better equipped to ask questions about their origins after doing a genogram.

The Wedding of Martin and Carmilla. Martin's father had been baptized in St. Andrew's Church. That is the reason he gave for wanting to be married there. Martin made the initial contact to line up the church for the wedding because Carmilla, who had been baptized a Roman Catholic, belonged to no church. Martin (age thirty) and Carmilla (age twenty-seven) did not think they needed the pre-wedding preparation the church required because she had been married before. They nonetheless agreed to pre-wedding conversations in which they would do genograms (see Figures 5 and 6), because they both wanted to be married at St. Andrew's.

Three things were significant about Martin's genogram. (1) His parents divorced when he was thirteen, and Martin was "abandoned" by them both to be raised by his father's mother whom he knew only as "Gram." She ran a loose household, with many foster children. Martin learned to fend for himself in order to survive. "Gram" was a generous and hospitable woman who loved children. (2) Martin learned a family secret only after he told "Gram" of his intention to marry. She had been married to a sailor she called Jeb, who was presumed dead in a shipwreck. She married again, to Ivan, and shortly thereafter Jeb reappeared and demanded his rightful role as husband. "Gram" would not be bullied, as she put it, and divorced the sailor. Martin could understand his own caution about marrying more clearly when he learned this secret. (3) Martin is isolated from his father because of a conflict with his father's second wife. He has seen his own mother (who now lives in another country) only three times since the divorce seventeen years ago.

FIGURE 5
Martin's Genogram

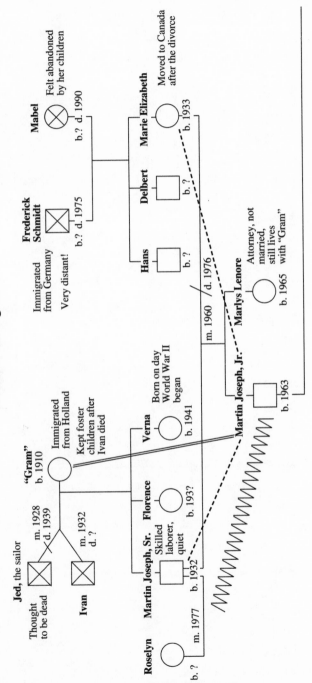

FIGURE 6
Carmilla's Genogram

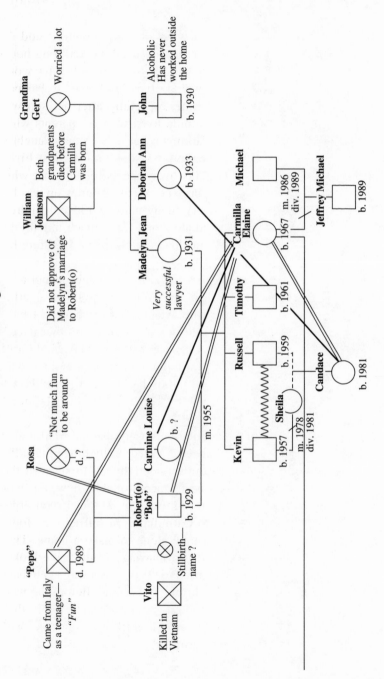

Carmilla was married when she was nineteen and divorced three years later. Her first husband worked long hours and kept even longer hours with his male friends after work. Carmilla reported that she would often "go home" to her parents for several days at a time, especially after her son was born. After her divorce, Carmilla lived with her parents while she finished trade school. Carmilla is her father's only daughter. Her father had a much younger sister who died at birth. Carmilla described her parents' marriage as friendly, but without much affection. Her favorite person as she grew up was her Grandpa Pepe. He was a very funny man who loved children. His wife was very quiet and aloof and "very much like my father," as Carmilla put it. Grandpa Pepe died shortly before her son Jeffrey was born.

The most dramatic story in Carmilla's family is not a secret, but it is an ongoing saga. Her brother Russell had an affair with their brother Kevin's wife, which occasioned a child and a divorce. The brothers still do not speak to each other except through Russell's daughter, Candace, who has been cared for by the grandparents until now. Carmilla often took care of Candace when she lived at home. The family has asked if Carmilla will care for Candace, who is now twelve, after she and Martin are married.

The pastoral conversation with Carmilla and Martin after the genograms were completed focused on the lingering influence of their origins. Carmilla is determined to succeed this time in making a home. She is uncomfortable, however, with the influence of "Gram" on Martin's life. Martin is concerned that if Candace is added to Carmilla's son Jeffrey (age four), they will not have enough time alone to make a home. They were invited to imagine what a marriage would have looked like if "Gram" had been married to "Pepe," as a way to envision the kind of family they might like to become. Before the wedding, they were able to decide not to take Candace into their home on a permanent basis, and Martin had a "big talk" with "Gram" about his love for Carmilla.[8]

Significant Themes to Explore

No two genograms are alike. Family stories are unique and so is each member's interpretation of those stories. The patterns of interacting across and within the generations, the values and traditions, and the legacy of roles, rules, and rituals are also particular to every family. There are, however, some common themes to look for in doing a genogram. We have organized them around the following series of questions. The way one approaches these themes will be different with each couple, because the responses to some of the first questions we ask will determine what particular areas it might be important to pursue. No single genogram exercise can or should be expected to cover all these questions.

1. *What are the patterns of closeness and distance among family members?* Do the parents have a close marriage? What stories are told about the marriage of grandparents? Which child is close to which parent? What are the alliances among siblings? What are the attitudes about intimacy and sexuality in the family? Did some people work together better than others? Has anyone had difficulty leaving home?

2. *Are there special alliances that include one or both parents and cross generational lines?* What is the primary triangle in the family system? Is there anyone who is a permanent outsider? How does the family handle the question of loyalty? Are there secret alliances? Is there a child or grandchild who is the recipient of a special blessing? Are there naming patterns that suggest the bestowal of particular blessings?

3. *Is the family open or closed to the world outside?* Does the family value privacy highly? How are outsiders welcomed into the family? Is it easy or hard to become a part of the family? Is the family involved in activities in the community or church or neighborhood? Is the family open to differences that children bring home in the form of friends or ideas?

4. *How were family beliefs and values expressed?* How were religious beliefs expressed? How were values taught? If your parents had different views on religion or politics, how

were those differences worked out? Can you identify the beliefs and values by how people worked and played, or by the organizations they belonged to? Were there sayings or family maxims that were frequently repeated by a parent or grandparent? What are the organizing myths that the family lives by?

5. *In what ways are cultural ethnic factors important to the family's history?* If there were differences between the ethnic traditions of parents or their families, how were those differences dealt with? In the marriage of your parents, which ethnic traditions predominated?

6. *What is the family's history of loss and grief?* Is there a pattern of buried grief? Are there births and deaths in close proximity? For example, did grandfather die six months before or after the youngest child was born? If two things happen in the same year, was there any other loss? When there are a series of deaths before a child is born, what does that mean for the child? One of the things that makes a genogram different from a family tree is the relationship of events. The juxtaposition of the death of a parent and the birth of a child is particularly difficult because those two events introduce the processes of celebrating and mourning, which are not easily compatible.[9]

7. *Are there repetitive symptoms, relationships, or functioning patterns across the family or over generations?* Are there losses that repeat generation after generation? What is the family's way of dealing with change? Are there patterns of failure that repeat? Is conflict unresolved or are resentments harbored? Is there a pattern of alcohol abuse or divorce or angry leaving-home events or unwanted pregnancies over time?

8. *What roles, rules, and rituals are part of the family legacy?* Who are the responsible ones? Is there a family peacemaker or scapegoat? What are some of the other roles? Is there one person that the family worries about? Does the person about to marry understand his or her role in the family? Are there special rituals in the family for the celebration of birthdays? How did the family enforce its values or beliefs? Were there, for example, rules posted on the refrigerator door?

9. *What are the strengths of the family?* What are the patterns of survival or coping with stress that are constructive? What are the things that have helped your family endure over time? It is especially important to lift up the positive signs gleaned from family stories that are regarded as negative without denying the reality of pain or struggle in the family.

10. *If you want to find out more about your family, who could you ask?* Who knows the family stories? Is there a family historian? Who keeps the secrets? Who would be willing to break a family rule to tell you what you need to know about your family in order to be better prepared to marry? These questions are particularly important when someone comes from a family in which stories are simply not told.

It cannot be emphasized enough that the aim of doing a genogram is not simply the gathering of data; it is the initiation of a process of storytelling that is intended to extend far beyond the time of the pastoral conversation. In the brief span of time usually available before the wedding, it is not possible to examine all the topics listed above. The most one can hope for is to foster in the couple a curiosity about their origins and initiate them into a mode of storytelling that will become a part of their process of becoming married.

A Sequence of Pre-wedding Meetings

The method of pre-wedding preparation we are proposing lends itself to a variety of patterns for meeting with the couple. If the preparation is spread over a long period of time, it may be possible to meet with a couple several times. If the method of preparation includes weekend retreats or conversations in a group setting, another pattern is likely to be followed. It is not likely that one can do justice to this process in less than three meetings with a couple after the initial meeting. In large parishes that have many weddings, this plan could be modified so that the pastor need not conduct all the meetings. The fourth meeting for planning the wedding liturgy does, however, require someone with developed skills in pastoral theological reflection. That is the primary focus of the next chapter.

The *first or initial meeting with the couple* is usually brief. The aim is to clarify some of the details surrounding the wedding. As a way of becoming acquainted with the couple, it is beneficial to trace the development of their relationship. As we have already noted, it is useful to explore with the couple how they have moved from a private to a more public relationship. The meeting with a minister to begin preparations for the wedding may in fact be another step in the process of "going public" with the relationship. For that reason, this meeting with the couple should be taken seriously even if it is brief. At the conclusion of the initial meeting, the process that will be used the next time will be described briefly. Sometimes it is enough to say that what you will do together is like making a family tree with stories added. The couple is again assured that no preparation is required.

The *second meeting with the couple* is devoted to doing their genograms. Because it is an almost infinitely expandable method, several sessions could be used to complete the work for a couple. However, it is possible, and even desirable, to complete both genograms in one meeting. That meeting may take as long as two hours, depending on how long it takes to tell the stories. While it will not be possible to explore all the material that some couples will know about their families in such a short time, others may know so little that an hour will be more than enough time. Even though one partner may have more stories to tell than the other, it is important to balance the time spent with each family of origin as a way of symbolizing parity between the two stories that are merging to form a new narrative.

In order to be evenhanded in one's response to the couple, whether one begins with the bride or groom should be determined in an arbitrary way. The danger is that the one who knows the most, or the family of origin the couple is most likely to be joining, or the one the pastor knows best will be the first family presented. Following the family system's principle of starting with whoever is farthest out might mean beginning with the family less well known by the other marital partner.

If preparation for the wedding is done in a group context, it is not possible to make a genogram of the family of each person in the group. One or two genograms are enough, however, to demonstrate the value of exploring one's origins for the sake of becoming married. In a larger group context, couples may do their own genograms, or work in partnership with other couples. In a group setting, other methods may be more useful in generating a similar awareness of family dynamics. In pairs (preferably not with spouse-to-be), people may be invited to *tell stories* about any of the themes that have been identified above. After such a rehearsal, and still within the group setting, couples may begin separately to identify the impact of those stories on the new family they intend to form and how they might together decide the future of their marriage.

The purpose of *the third meeting* is to explore with the couple the implications for their marriage of what they have learned about their family legacies. It is important to wait to make those connections. If we push prematurely for parallels between their families of origin and their present relationship, we risk diminishing the nonthreatening atmosphere that a genogram creates. Ideally, both the individual partners and the couple will use time between the first genogram meeting and a later discussion of connections to make their own discoveries.

In this follow-up conversation, the focus still remains on each family of origin, even though the questions shift to the new family the couple is beginning to form. The conversation is likely to begin with some exploration of information they may have received, or stories they may have heard, that helped to fill in the empty places in the genogram. The primary task of this meeting, however, is *to help the couple see more clearly their relationship to each other in the light of their relationships to their families of origin.* There are at least four questions that provide a framework for the discussion.

1. *What is there about your family of origin that you want to be sure to include in the new family you are forming?* Our

intent is to be explicit about the ways in which they may want to recapitulate their first-family experience. In a way, it is like collecting the emotional "dowry" of attitudes, traditions, and patterns of interacting that each person would like to contribute to the new family that is being formed. Sometimes this discussion will also provide the occasion for practicing the art of compromise if the expectations are in conflict.

2. *What is there about your family of origin that you would not like to continue in this new family?* For some people, this is easier to answer than the previous question. The experience of their parents' marriage or their own place in the family is filled with so much pain that they cannot imagine continuing anything. What is tricky about such a response is that it may mask an "emotional cutoff" from one's family of origin. This is particularly true if an individual denies all influence and rejects any present or future contacts with his or her family. Such a disposition is an indication that the person may not have left home enough to become married.

3. *Who or what will make it difficult to leave the family you come from and who or what will make it easy for you to become married?* This question may require some prompting. Sometimes it is helpful to look again at the marriage of the individual's parents to see how they did it. Becoming married may be helped or hindered by significant people in their lives. Usually those people are part of family. Sometimes it is children from a previous marriage or a former father-in-law who is still grandfather to your children who will make becoming married difficult. As the boundaries between family and nonfamily become more fluid, it is possible that friends may also play a significant role in enhancing or impeding the process of becoming married.

> Lucinda and I both came from violent homes. Even before I was big enough, it was my job to protect my mother from my father. Lucinda had been beaten as a child by her father. I knew that Lucinda was attracted to my strength. I didn't know that she was afraid of my temper until she told that to the pastor who was going to marry us. It made

me mad that she brought it up in front of the pastor, and I told her so. I still don't understand why she cried, because I have promised not to hurt her. The pastor suggested that we had some things to work through before we should think of marriage. I got another minister to do the wedding who didn't interfere. We were really lucky to get a trailer in the same area where my mom lives so I can keep an eye on her. (Clayton)

For couples like Lucinda and Clayton, becoming married is likely to be impeded by the expectations and roles from their families of origin that each is repeating: Clayton as the protector and Lucinda as the one needing protecting. For other couples, it may be work patterns or the demands of school or the presence of children or an anticipated separation shortly after the wedding or living circumstances that will hinder the process of becoming married. If it is possible to identify these impediments clearly, it will help the couple determine the work they need to do together to make the marriage work. For that reason, there is yet one more question to ask.

4. *What can you do as a couple to assist each other in the process of becoming married?* For some this may mean support for the leaving-home process. Being married enhances the process of leaving home because we have an ally to support us when we take an anxiety-producing stand with our parents. People who have difficulty leaving home need to be careful to do the work of differentiating for themselves, especially when they think their spouse has more courage for the task than they do. It is easy enough to *say* that becoming married is hard work. It is more difficult and more important to be specific about the kind of work that needs to be done or not done.

Some Gatekeeping Is Inevitable

The purpose of our work with couples prior to the wedding is not just to enhance the leaving-home process or to increase their understanding of family legacies. It is to point to the goodness of

God's love, which is revealed in a partial way in the love that motivates people to marry. People in love are frequently surprised by a kind of love they have not known before. Whenever two people marry, God is doing something new. We may not see it. We may even try to impede it. If a couple and/or their families are determined to make a new family just like the old ones, then it is difficult for God to be doing a new thing.

The focus on understanding our origins is to clear impediments to forming a new family. It is a way of preparing for marriage that avoids directly evaluating the relationship. The hope is rather that the couple might discover for themselves areas of potential difficulty in their relationship as they think about it in the light of their family origins. If an immediate marriage is unwise, it is obviously best if the couple themselves decide to postpone the wedding or not to marry at all in the light of that knowledge.

> Neither Dianna nor Bill was a member of my church, but I was glad to work with them before their wedding. It was a form of service and a way of doing evangelism in our small town with one church and one pastor. They were not eager to do the genogram, nor were they interested in reading what I suggested. But they came to the sessions and told family stories with mildly growing interest. As we talked together, it became clearer to me than to them that both families were extremely patriarchal and one was both physically and psychologically abusive. The genogram proved pivotal, because it was the occasion to talk about how their families spent leisure time. Bowling was a common hobby and had brought them together. Dianna discovered that besides bowling, Bill was mostly interested in watching sports on TV. His idea of a perfect evening at home was a couple of beers and the sports channel and a little sex at the end. They did not come back to see me after that conversation. Several weeks later I saw Dianna in the supermarket, and she informed me that the wedding was off.   (Pastor Beck)

There are, however, some circumstances in which a minister may decide not to participate in a wedding ceremony for a couple. We mention them here to recognize that there is an inevitable gatekeeping function in all pre-wedding work.

—When the couple has no interest in exploring the relationship of their own family stories to the Christian story, there may be good reason to suggest that being married in a church may not be appropriate. Helping the couple to be clear about the place of religion in their life is one way to make the beginning of their life together as authentic as possible.

—The church may say no to a couple who is unwilling or unable to participate in whatever process of preparation is required prior to the wedding. In order to avoid misunderstanding on what is required, it is most helpful for a church to have a written policy statement about weddings and wedding preparation.

—If there is indication of deceit or of sufficient character disorder to impair the ability to make commitments or keep promises, a minister may decide not to participate.

—Any sign that one will do harm to the other is cause for concern. This will be a particularly significant factor to attend to if there is a history of abuse from either family of origin.

The emphasis of most premarital programs or inventories is on assisting couples to evaluate their relationship in order to (*a*) determine areas of strength *and* potential conflict, and (*b*) engage the couple in conversations about critical areas in their relationship. The focus is on the couple and the potential of their relationship to fulfill the range of demands that will be made on them. Although psychological gatekeeping is not the primary purpose of these inventories, it is difficult to avoid evaluating the relationship when the potential conflicts are clearly identified through the inventory process.

Conclusion

The intent of our approach to prewedding preparation has been to foster an atmosphere of willing exploration into the lingering significance of the families of our origin. For some, this will mean a more determined effort to gain enough emotional separation from those families to make a commitment to marry. For others, this family exploration will aim at understanding the legacy of values and patterns of interacting that each one brings to the task of forming a new family and how that legacy is likely to continue to affect their process of becoming married.

This approach can be distinguished from other perspectives on premarital preparation in four respects: (1) It uses the genogram as the method of inquiry rather than a personality inventory. (2) The focus on the relationship of the couple is primarily in the light of connections made with the legacies of their families of origin. (3) Teaching about the meaning of marriage is done primarily in the context of planning the wedding. (4) Issues about relationship ordinarily dealt with in premarital counseling are examined more effectively after the wedding. For that reason, this pre-wedding approach presumes that the church will provide opportunities *after* the wedding for "in-service education" for couples in the process of becoming married.

Most couples want their marriage to be something new and special even if they do not know exactly how to make that possible. The pastoral task before the wedding is to help the couple be clear about the legacies they bring from their families of origin and how those families might continue to make claims on them. It is equally important, however, to help the couple envision the kind of family they want to become. The wedding occurs between the claims of the past *and* the claims of a future that pulls us forward to something new. We turn next to this work of planning a wedding, which usually occurs in the *fourth meeting with the couple.*

3
PLANNING A
MEANINGFUL WEDDING

EVERYONE HAS a favorite wedding story. We will remember the outdoor ceremony that had to be
stopped when insects attacked the wedding party. Or the wedding with full orchestra that resembled a coronation. Or the
wedding that was delayed because the groom, who was eighty-
two, had forgotten his teeth. Or the simple Quaker service that
began and ended in silence. Or the wedding couple that separated before the reception was over. Or the wedding reception
that lasted two days because of a blizzard.

Sometimes we remember most what was missing. The
ceremony had a wooden feel to it; nobody seemed very happy;
the words of promise were forced and anxious; the pomp and
splendor did not cover a sense of emptiness; the minister was
overbearing and competing for center stage. We may leave
weddings feeling indifferent or slightly sad or even a little irri-
tated and not know why.

There are other weddings, however, that touch people in a
deep and personal way. They open us to the joy and pain of our
own marriage or they touch the longing in our souls for the
companionship of another person. We remember the promises
we have made and broken. We are reminded again of the persistent love of family and the faithfulness of God. At those weddings everyone, not just the marrying couple, is blessed.

Beth and John had worked hard to plan a wedding that re-
spected the very different traditions of their origins. They
wanted to "do it well" so that everyone would be happy,
but it had not been easy. Whatever could go wrong had
gone wrong. And yet they seemed to survive the planning
process with good humor and a deepened appreciation of
each other. The service was not as flawless as they had
hoped. But when Beth and John spoke their vows, the
mood shifted. Whatever else had happened, this moment
was theirs and flaws were irrelevant. They spoke out of
their young souls with a kind of love and wisdom that was
authentic. Their promises embodied a recognition of the
struggles they had experienced and the genuine hopeful-
ness that comes from facing reality. There was an authenticity to their promises that could not be faked. We were
all blessed by their blessing of each other.   (Cotton)

Beth and John's wedding was memorable not because of perfect
planning or elegant ambiance but because of their genuine intent to become married. Their promises made promising believ-
able. When that kind of authenticity is present, weddings are
more like parable than myth.

The Needs for Planning

This chapter is about a pastoral approach to planning the
wedding. In the schema that we are proposing, conversation
with the couple about the wedding itself will take place in the
fourth meeting between the minister and the couple. It occurs
after using a genogram to explore families of origin and then
conversing with the couple about their emerging relationship
in the light of those families. The context for planning the
wedding is therefore wider than their relationship. The sequence is not accidental. It is an extension of the emphasis on
the wedding as public commitment by the couple, in the midst
of their significant communities, that they intend to become
married.[1]

The importance of planning the ritual as a part of pre-wedding work is a consequence of at least three related factors. There is, first of all, a growing recognition of the need to recover symbol and ritual in human life.[2] The growing complexity of our lives increases the need for rituals of transition. That need extends beyond the process of becoming married, but certainly includes it. The wedding is a ceremony that negotiates power and realigns relationships for a wide range of people. Meaningful rituals are as crucial for making a marriage as the moral seriousness of the couple.

In a study of marrying and burying, Ronald Grimes has described the need for ritual in this way:

> No matter how deeply couples "share" on retreats or learn, under priestly or therapeutic guidance, to "talk through" everything, they are not prepared to wed until their insights are somatized, made flesh, in ritual. It is a mistake to assume that couples automatically incarnate their own insights, just as it is courting disaster to relegate the work of embodying to the bedroom.[3]

This is a bold word with which we agree. Our marriages are seldom different from the rites with which they begin. Becoming married is a process that surely takes time, but how we begin matters very much.

The second factor that mandates more careful attention to planning the liturgy as part of pre-wedding work is that most religious traditions allow and even encourage the couple to participate in planning their own wedding ceremony. As we will suggest later in this chapter, there are some standard elements for a ritual that occurs in the context of Christian community. Within those parameters, however, the couple is encouraged to plan a liturgy that reflects their values and the vision of family toward which they would like to grow. Even when there are differences regarding the religious meaning *of* marriage, it is both possible and necessary for couples to find common themes from the Christian tradition *for* family living.

The third element that supports this perspective on pre-wedding work is the widespread longing to recover the distinctly pastoral dimension of the church's ministry. As we noted in the previous chapter, most of the categories used to counsel couples prior to marriage have been drawn from psychological resources. We do not wish to return to an earlier pattern of premarital pastoral work in which catechesis was the dominant mode and human process was ignored. The model for pre-wedding work presented here takes seriously what we have learned from family systems theory about becoming married as a process. It suggests a way for couples to identify the values from their faith traditions that might express the vision of family they intend to become. And it encourages couples to plan a celebration of fidelity that initiates a process *and* effects a new reality for the couple and for the community of their friends.

The Wedding as a Rite of Passage

The wedding is a ritual event that occurs in the midst of a process that has two parts: leaving home and becoming married. Sometimes the wedding is *the* leaving-home event, or at least close enough to that process that leaving-home issues dominate the wedding. In some instances, the work of becoming married is delayed until one or both partners in marriage have emotionally left home.

> Samantha and I were married when we were both twenty-one. We had dated for only a short time. Samantha did not want a big wedding because she and her parents were not on good terms. Samantha had told me that her parents had always been on her case about bad grades and disobeying the family rules. In her last year of high school, she ran away from home in order to have enough freedom to grow. I had troubles with my parents too. They divorced when I was twelve, and nothing was the same again. Before the wedding Samantha and I were together all the

time. Six weeks after the wedding, all of a sudden Samantha and her mother became great friends and I went to
movies alone. I wish we had waited to get married. (Kirk)

For very different reasons, both Kirk and Samantha had unresolved issues around separating from their families of origin
that needed to be worked through before the bonds of marriage
could begin to hold. By marrying Samantha, Kirk hoped to find
a home he hadn't had since boyhood, but Samantha was not
ready for that task because she had not emotionally left home
yet. Making friends with her mother was her next step so that
Samantha could eventually make a genuine emotional separation. Kirk had reconnecting work to do with his divorced family
of origin as well, so that he might make a marriage rather than
find a substitute home. Pre-wedding conversations about their
families might not have forestalled the crisis that occurred after
six weeks of marriage, but it would have helped the couple understand its origins.

The wedding and all the rituals that surround it are a *rite
of passage* from the social status of being single to that of
being married. In his work on wedding rituals, Kenneth W.
Stevenson reminds us that the modern marriage liturgies com-
bine what were separate rites until the end of the Middle
Ages.[4] The betrothal was the rite of separation, which initiated
a time of engagement. It was distinct from the rite of incorporation, the celebration of marriage. The modern wedding ceremony is a blend of both rites, although the emphasis is more
clearly on incorporation and joining.

Because a wedding embodies both leaving and cleaving,
it would be useful to recover something of the connection between the rite of separation and the rite of connection. There
are at least two ritual choices. We can reinstate the rite of betrothal as a separate and earlier moment that symbolizes the
leaving home that has happened and is happening for each
individual anticipating marriage. This ritualization of the leaving-

home process would give new meaning to publishing the banns. The second option would be to plan a wedding ritual that reflects both of the processes. The latter is more likely, because it is difficult to imagine reconstituting the betrothal rite in modern, mobile societies. One possibility would be to create a ceremony for the parental blessing of children that may be added to the wedding itself or celebrated around the time of the wedding rehearsal.[5]

The word that is most frequently used to describe this time of transition between separation and the incorporation of the wedding is *liminality*. In his classic work on *The Rites of Passage*, van Gennep maintains that "the passage from one social position to another is identified with a territorial passage, such as the entrance into a village or a house, the movement from one room to another, or the crossing of streets and squares."[6] In traditional cultures, marriage involved an actual change from one family, clan, village, or tribe to another. It was a territorial passage with social consequences.

During this transitional or liminal time, participants in the process are temporarily without social status and rank. This temporary loss of identity often results in confusion. In order to ensure some stability in the midst of the chaos and anonymity of a liminal time, there are prescribed forms of dress or behavior. It is not surprising, therefore, that people who are nontraditional in every other aspect of their lives will insist on very traditional dress and symbolic action as part of the wedding.

The benefit of understanding the liminal character of the wedding event is that it helps people anticipate the inevitable stress it evokes. Getting married ushers in an in-between time, a time in which the old status as a single person is no longer entirely true but the new status has not yet been bestowed or internalized. It is an inherently confusing and, therefore, a stressful time. It is a time when people are most vulnerable, when the blemishes (and more serious dysfunctions) are likely to show, and when self-reflection is particularly difficult. One way that people cope with the chaos is to plan weddings that are picture-perfect.

The wedding is ordinarily an emotionally charged moment. It is more so if the leaving-home work is still unfinished. Even those who have lived apart from their homes of origin or lived together as a couple are surprised by the intensity of the emotions around planning a wedding. The situation is further complicated by separate portfolios and careers and separate furnishings and pension plans that must be merged in a responsible and just way. What makes the time around a wedding so difficult for everyone is that major transitions are taking place in a person's identity and a family's stability. It is like maneuvering between two boats in choppy waters. Few of us are surefooted at such times. We need rituals of transition that acknowledge the reality of contradiction and chaos at this liminal time. We need weddings that are more like parable than myth.

Discovering a Theme for the Wedding

We are indebted to Nico ter Linden, the pastor of the Westerkirk in Amsterdam, the Netherlands, for introducing us to a process by which couples are invited to discover a theme for the wedding and the marriage it inaugurates. Although ter Linden has developed his approach within a social context that is thoroughly secular, the method works equally well within a framework in which religious symbols or traditional Christian stories and values are still part of the common culture. The task is to identify an image or theme that can be used to link the narrative the couple is forming from their many stories with *the* Christian story.[7]

The process actually begins at the conclusion of the meeting with the couple that immediately precedes the one in which the focus is on planning the wedding. Each individual is invited to think about stories or songs or plays or movies or sayings *from any source* that convey something about their hope for the family they are forming. The emphasis is on *their* hopes or dreams more than the source of the image or story. For that reason, anything can serve as a place to begin. The selection of scriptural texts may be a springboard for this discussion. The pastoral task is to find a way to move from those images to themes and stories from the Christian tradition that will reflect and undergird the kind of family they hope to become.

> When Isabel came to the meeting with Erik and myself to think together about a theme for their wedding, she was very uncomfortable. She had been unable to think of anything. The only story Isabel could remember from the Bible was the feeding of the five thousand. After some time of careful exploration, Isabel was able to acknowledge that she was afraid that she would not "have enough" to sustain her relationship with Erik. She did not doubt her love for Erik (or his love for her), but she was afraid that eventually she would "run out of love." When she thought of the possibility of having children, she surely would not have enough "loaves and fishes" to provide for the emotional nurture of her children. And she certainly did not expect that God would make enough so that there would be leftovers. We made the story of Jesus feeding the five thousand (Matt. 14:13–21) the focal point of lessons and prayers of the wedding liturgy and, although she remained fearful, Isabel was able to entertain the possibility that maybe her life with Erik would be one of God's miracles.
>
> (Nico ter Linden)

Developing a theme or image that anticipates the kind of family the marrying couple would like to become is a way of linking the stories from families of origin with the Christian story. This means learning to weave one's individual, familial, and future marital story with the narrative of God's redeeming work in Jesus Christ. It will be awkward for some couples who have never thought about their story in relation to God's story. For that reason, we use planning the wedding ritual as a tool, like the genogram, to invite the couple to explore ways in which they might envision their life together in the light of the Christian story. Ultimately this means an invitation into a relationship with the God whose presence these rites mediate.

As the couple's preparation for the wedding proceeds and aspects of their personal and family stories begin to unfold, certain values, commitments, and life themes will quite naturally become evident. As they do, even before the conversation about planning the liturgy, these themes can help shape the larger wedding ceremony in a way that honors each individual's past and anticipates the couple's common future. Some themes will develop out of families of origin. Others will become apparent from the couple's own history. Still others will embody the faith traditions of the couple.

> Both my daughter Joy and her husband, Gilbert, have said that selecting what to include in the booklet they gave the wedding guests was the best preparation they did for their life together. One of my favorite quotes from the booklet is a sentence from the poet and essayist Rainer Maria Rilke in *Rilke on Love and Other Difficulties*: "Once the realization is accepted that even between the closest human beings infinite distances continue to exist, a wonderful living side by side can grow up, if they succeed in loving the distance between them which makes it possible for each to see the other whole and against a wide sky."[8]   (Herbert)

The image of being married as "loving the distance between them" is consistent with the paradoxical approach we have taken to marriage throughout this volume. In an earlier chapter, we suggested that parable is a more accurate telling of the Christian story than myth. It is also better preparation for marriage because it acknowledges that contradiction or paradox is an inevitable dimension of faithful living and an inescapable reality of family living. The stories or images or sayings that a couple presents initially may not always reflect this understanding of marriage. For that reason, pre-wedding pastoral work may need to include "saying the other side," so that the themes that a couple finally chooses will be consistent with the parabolic way of Jesus. We have identified three contradictions that are present in wedding preparation but also characteristic of being married.

Continuity and Discontinuity

The first and most obvious paradox of becoming married is reflected in the simultaneous beginnings and endings, the continuities and discontinuities, that characterize every wedding. The wedding launches a new adventure, that of becoming married. At the same time, it brings to a close a host of possibilities that were part of being single. We leave elements of our personal history behind, and yet nothing ever really leaves us. It is simply transformed at a deeper level. The wedding as we have it today has condensed two distinct ritual processes of separation and incorporation into one event. It is about leaving as well as cleaving.

In the new version of the old classic film *Father of the Bride*, the father awakes to discover his daughter bride-to-be shooting baskets in the driveway. In a wonderfully tender conversation that describes the paradox of holding on and letting go, the daughter says this to her father: "I just kept thinking about how this is my last night in my bed, and kind of like my last night as a kid. I mean, I've lived here since I was five—and I feel like I'm supposed to turn in my key tomorrow. It was so strange packing up my room. You know how you always trained me never to throw things away? I couldn't throw anything away, so I have all these yearbooks and ratty stuffed animals, my old retainer, all my old magic tricks. I've actually packed it all. I just couldn't let go. I mean, I know I can't stay, but I don't want to leave."

There are a variety of patterns for leaving and letting go. Sometimes parents are ready to let go before children are ready to leave. Other times parents hold on to children who are ready to leave. This is *the* psychological drama of a wedding. If the process is allowed to unfold in a parabolic way, there *can* be a giving up and a getting at the same time. We need to develop wedding rituals in which parental and family relationships are acknowledged and honored at the same time they are symbolically severed.

Bonds and Boundaries

The second paradox is about bonds and boundaries, connectedness and separateness. It is a theme that we have explored throughout this essay and that will continue to be a foundational concept for the entire series on Family Living in Pastoral Perspective. Rilke is right. One of the greatest gifts we can give those to whom we are married is to love the distance between us. The wedding ritual, however, has all too frequently emphasized being "one flesh" at the expense of honoring human separateness. The focus of a wedding is on the process of bonding that is being intended by the couple, and that is as it should be. Unless, however, an individual marrying has sufficiently left to establish clear and flexible boundaries in relation to family of origin, that bonding may come eventually to feel like suffocation or invasion.

People marrying after living on their own want to be assured that they will not lose their hard-won sense of self in the process. The wedding liturgy needs to give expression to these polarities, which will characterize the long process of becoming married that is only now beginning. Again Rilke has said it well: "It is a question in marriage, to my feeling, not of creating a quick community of spirit by tearing down and destroying all boundaries, but rather a good marriage is that which appoints the other guardian of his solitude, and shows him this confidence, the greatest in his power to bestow."[9]

Private Event, Public Context

The wedding is a public event that celebrates, at least in most cultures, a private, voluntary covenant. This third paradox of the wedding also describes the entire process of becoming and being married. We have already suggested that making public the private decision to marry may, in some instances, be another leaving-home moment. In every instance, how a couple negotiates this transition from private relationship to public status is a significant part of becoming married. The rituals that precede a wedding, such as showers or engagement parties, support this movement from private to public. They enable the communities of family and friends of the couple to recognize their new public status. We need to find more and more ways to emphasize the public nature of marriage.

The corollary of making marriage more public is for the public sphere to take on qualities of recognition and nurturance previously confined to the private sphere of the family. A marriage needs to be private enough to provide a safe place for individual selves to be sustained and intimacy to be nurtured. Those values cannot be sustained, however, if they belong only to the private sphere of the family. The family cannot alone sustain qualities like nurture and recognition if the public world is defined as a place in which care for others is impossible and atomized selves protect their autonomy by denying the reality of others. Those who would keep the traditional split between the private, female world of nurture and the public, male world of achievement are likely to insist on keeping marriage private.

Marriage is a sign of God's love and faithfulness, but it is also a place from which we are sent to serve the world for God's sake. People who rarely close their doors find little occasion to nurture intimacy; those who rarely open them run the risk of deadening self-absorption and perpetuating a society that cannot support family living. If the wedding ritual is to enhance a more fluid relationship between public and private worlds, it will always be paradoxical. We have suggested ways in which the paradox of leaving and cleaving may be reflected in the wedding ceremony itself. It will be equally necessary to balance the public and private realities of becoming married.

Common Elements of a Wedding Liturgy

The elements of the wedding liturgy we have chosen to highlight may not be immediately recognizable to all readers because of the diversity of religious traditions. Some elements of the marriage liturgy are open for adaptation according to the rules for each church; others are not. There are enough options, however, for personalizing a wedding service to warrant the time of the pastor and the couple invested in planning. It is at the same time a significant opportunity to deepen the couple's understanding of themselves, their faith, and the vision of family that will sustain the hard work of becoming married.

The Greeting

The liturgy begins with the pastor's invitation to the assembly to bear witness to and bless this couple who make public declaration of their intent to become married. This is also a reminder of the significance of marriage itself, which is reinforced by reference to Jesus at the wedding at Cana of Galilee. The greeting declares the frame in which the couple's pledge to become married will occur. Two people who marry not only commit themselves to each other; they make a pledge to treat the institution of marriage with the respect and reverence it is due.

There are numerous renditions of the words of invitation and exhortation from which the couple may adapt and choose, but the significance of the greeting should not be overlooked. What is done following the greeting is done in the name of God. The German theologian Dietrich Bonhoeffer wrote this in a wedding sermon from his prison cell:

> Your love is your private possession, but marriage is more than something personal—it is a status, an office. Just as it is the crown, and not merely the will to rule, that makes the king, so it is marriage, and not merely your love for each other, that joins you together in the sight of God and one another.[10]

One way to include the ritual elements of a betrothal rite in the wedding ceremony is to mark the transition of leaving at the beginning of the ceremony. The opening greeting is done with the family and significant friends around the couple. Following the greeting, those surrounding the couple may express a blessing as a parent to a son or daughter, make a wish for happiness as a friend, rejoice as a sibling to have a room alone, or offer as an aunt or uncle the promise of support and ongoing prayers. The purpose of the ritual moment is to dramatize separating from families of origin and friends in order to be free to marry. When the blessings are ended, the presider will invite the family and friends and the wedding party to leave the couple standing alone to make their pledge to marry.

Declaration of Intent

In one form of the marriage service, the minister invites the couple "in the presence of God and these people, to declare your intention to enter into union with one another through the grace of Jesus Christ." Usually the minister then asks each one if he or she will love and comfort and honor and keep the other in sickness and health until death, and they each answer more or less audibly, "I will." It is not always clear to whom the "I will" is addressed. Out of awkwardness, they may look at each other or the minister or the candles on the altar. Their declaration of intent, however, is as much for the congregation as for each other. Because of the public nature of this moment, it is as important as the vow that follows.

In order to strengthen this moment in which the couple makes a public pledge of their intention to become married, two things would be helpful: (1) that each one say the entire declaration rather than simply answer "I will" and (2) that they address the assembly with what they say. When the declaration of intent is clearly stated to the assembly, it is easier for the assembly to respond with equal vigor with its promise to uphold these two persons who in this ceremony embark on the difficult and joyful process of becoming married. We return to this important theme of intentionality in the final chapter. It should be noted, however, that we take very seriously the promises of the assembly to support in their endeavor to become married. We cannot become or remain married without *both* intentionality *and* supportive communities.

Ministry of the Word

In most contemporary liturgies, reading from the scriptures is at the center between the declaration of intent to marry and the vows. The placement is significant because it suggests one more moment of reflection before the vows are taken. There are a range of appropriate passages from either testament from which the couple may choose one or more readings (see Appendix B). The previous discussion of themes for the wedding should provide a focus for the selection of scripture readings. It is also possible that the selection of texts to be read is a place to begin conversation about themes by which the couple might envision their life together. The couple may read passages from scripture or literature to one another. Reading lessons is one way for family and friends to participate in the wedding liturgy. The possibility of including nonbiblical readings in this time of reflection will depend on the policies of the local congregation or denomination. A pastor who is skilled in theological reflection will be able to make valuable connections between the family stories that a couple has told and the readings they choose for the wedding liturgy.

A wedding homily in response to the readings and the separate stories that are being forged into one narrative is optional but encouraged. If it is used wisely, the homily is a wonderful opportunity to help the couple recognize their story in the larger Christian story. The couple may not later remember what is said, but they are sure to remember what is done. Because of the vulnerability of the moment, the wedding homily is a special moment of intimacy between the presiding minister and the couple which the assembly is invited to overhear. The wedding homily is a time for pastoral reflection rather than theological exposition or moral admonition. It is an opportunity to allow the personal and family histories of the couple being married to mingle with the stories of faith. Both are illuminated when scripture intersects with human and social realities. And if it is done right, all those in the assembly who are or have been married should recognize themselves.

The Exchange of Vows

This is a relatively brief and simple moment in the liturgy. It is framed by the reflection on scripture that precedes it and the prayers of the community that follow. Some couples will prefer to rely on the traditional words for their vows; others may wish to craft the vows in their own words. If the vows are written by the couple, they should contain two elements that are essential to a Christian understanding of the marriage covenant: *faithfulness in all circumstances, and for the duration of life*. It is assumed that the vows are a continuation of the many promises that the couple have made to each other during the time of courtship preceding the wedding.

The exchange of vows is one of the most intimate private moments that a couple will ever share in public. For this moment, the couple face each other and the assembly overhears what is said. Some couples have memorized their vows as a way to symbolize the reality that the bride and groom are the primary liturgists of their own wedding, making the most significant promises of their lifetimes. By wrapping a stole around the hands of the husband and wife now joined together, the presiding minister may enact the belief that God promises not to undo what the couple has done. In order that the assembly also declares the couple married, it may respond in one voice: "We unite you and bind you to one another. We pronounce you husband and wife. Live in peace."[11] The exchange of vows is the emotional climax of the wedding liturgy. It is an appropriate moment for a doxology or hymn of celebration.

Prayers and Blessings

Once the marriage vows have been said in that public-private moment, the liturgy opens again to involve the community through prayer. Family and friends are invited to give voice to the blessings that come from God. With the nuptial blessing, the prayers often have the effect of a fountain pouring continuously over the couple, surrounding them with God's promise of constant love and graciousness. The prayers are not just for the newly married couple, but for all couples and families everywhere. Family and friends join in the prayers. If some participants have never prayed in public, they should be encouraged to practice reading aloud what is written in order to diminish anxiety and keep the focus on the prayer's meaning.

Prayer that is open to God and to the deepest desires of the human heart is a gift to the new couple—but also a moment of danger. Talking with the couple about which prayers to use in the service is another opportunity for the minister to help them identify what they hope for.

> The pastor who married us asked, somewhat facetiously, if he should pray the "fertility prayer" at our wedding. I said yes, because I wanted children. Jodie said absolutely not! Although we had talked vaguely about having children, and I thought she had vaguely agreed with the idea, it was not clear to me until three weeks before the wedding that she had no intention of having children. We should have stopped there. Instead, we were divorced three years later because I wanted to have children and she didn't.
> (Dale)

It is important, as Dale discovered, to be able to pray for what we want and to be clear that what we want is something we can pray for. Prayers that include our doubts and struggles add the authenticity of a ritual that does not exclude life's messiness. It would not have been appropriate for the pastor to pray that Dale wanted babies but Jodie did not, but naming the ambiguity about having children would have been helpful. When the couple can be clear about what they hope their life together will be, the prayers are a private as well as a public expression of the deep desires of the heart.

The community that gathers at the invitation of the couple who are marrying is there to celebrate and to bless. Every wedding ritual includes prayers for blessing, most of which are designated to be said by the presiding minister on behalf of the community. What is often missing, except for an occasional applause at the conclusion of the vows, is an opportunity for the community to say its blessing, to surround the couple with its joy, and to overwhelm the couple with the words and symbols of God's blessing. We suggest the following model for a marriage litany as a way for *the community to speak its blessing* to the couple for their life together and in the world.

Assembly:
God the Eternal keep you faithful to each other,
so that the peace of Christ may abide in your home.

Single voice:
May God bless you in your work and your companionship;
in your sleeping and in your waking.
May you have true friends to stand by you
in your joys and in your sorrows;
in your life and in your death.

Assembly:
God the Eternal keep you faithful to each other,
so that the peace of Christ may abide in your home.

Single voice:
Serve God and your neighbor in all that you do.
Bear witness to the love of God in this world,
so that those to whom love is a stranger
will find in you generous friends.

Assembly:
God the Eternal keep you faithful to each other,
so that the peace of Christ may abide in your home.

Eucharistic Celebration

Every expression of human love finds its source in God's love, and the Eucharist recalls and reenacts the essential movement of God to humanity. Not all traditions include the Eucharist as part of the marriage liturgy. If, however, the Eucharist is understood as the church's primary act of thanksgiving, it offers an excellent opportunity for the couple and the assembly to give expression of their gratitude to God. In the eucharistic meal, we remember and represent God's presence and God's promise of fidelity. The promise of the marital covenant echoes this divine intention.

Since the common table is so close to the heart of married life, the place to which we return day after day to nourish ourselves and remember the day that has passed, it is particularly appropriate as a symbol for the marital celebration. Breaking bread together and sharing a cup of wine recalls to us the holiness that is at the heart of our common life together. When the newly married couple are the eucharistic ministers, they have another opportunity to be hosts at the celebration of their marriage. Sharing bread and wine as a "love feast" may also occur as a moment in the celebration that follows.

> We wanted to involve as many members of our family as we could in the eucharistic meal at our wedding ceremony. Tom's sisters dressed the altar with a tablecloth that had been used by Tom's grandparents for festive meals. The plate for the bread was from Catherine's great-grandparents and the goblets for the wine were gifts to us from Catherine's parents. The antique candleholders that were placed on the altar by a niece and a nephew were gifts to our parents. Other members of our families presented the bread and wine that was used for the eucharistic meal. We wanted to intertwine the stories of our families with the story of the Eucharist to symbolize that God is at the center of our family. It was an honor for us to be eucharistic ministers. (Tom and Catherine)

Table Fellowship at the Rehearsal and the Reception

It is easy to understand from Tom and Catherine's story how the rehearsal dinner and the reception following the wedding ceremony may be a continuous expression of table fellowship. The table is again the common element at each occasion. It is symbolic of the table at the center of family living: where we nourish ourselves and disclose or disguise the realities of our lives; where we spread out the bills and income-tax forms and argue about who spends too much; where we gather with friends to be sustained in the journey; where we gather to order the disorder of our meeting and missing, our comings and goings; and where we gather to celebrate holy occasions of sacred and secular significance. It is at the table where hospitality must abide.

> To the best of my remembrance, over the last forty-eight years of marriage, Martha and I have never had a meal alone or with friends without lighting a candle. The tradition began at our wedding. The electricity went out at the recessional, so we had the reception by candlelight only. It was a wonderful moment. In that moment, we felt surrounded by the love of family and friends. We determined that night to make our table a place of warmth and hospitality for "all sorts and conditions." No matter how humble the meal, the candle lights up our lives and reminds us of the love that has knit us together through the years.   (Clarence)

Plans for the rehearsal, the rehearsal dinner, and the reception need to be guided by the table that stands at the center of each. Hospitality has little to do with money and everything to do with attitude. At the rehearsal, the pastor and the couple need to remember that they are hosting a group, many of whom will be strangers to one another. People will wonder how they will be recognized and how they will belong. Everyone is a little anxious. Many agendas crowd the stage. It is important to create an atmosphere in which everyone feels welcomed.

The rehearsal dinner is another opportunity for hospitality to flourish. There may be a few last-minute details to attend to, but most of the preparations and most of the worry are over. It is a time for toasting and storytelling. It is a time to express love and gratitude, to say goodbye and hello, to laugh and cry a bit, to further the cleaving (separation) for the sake of cleaving (bonding). Because everyone is a little more open, the entire wedding process holds the potential for mending wounded relationships and creating new levels of intimacy and connectedness.

> I had not spoken to my sister Denise for five years. Not since my divorce. The time of my divorce was very painful for me. The family's response to my pain had been to freeze me out because there I was, the first one in the family to get a divorce. I decided to accept the invitation to Joan's wedding because she had always been my favorite niece. But I dreaded seeing her straitlaced mother. I was prepared for more judgment. Since I came from out of town, Joan had insisted that I come to the rehearsal dinner. When Joan hugged me and told me how much it meant to her that I came, I cried. When Denise hugged me, I cried again. I was very glad to be reconnected.   (Carolyn)

Carolyn's story, repeated over and over again at weddings, points to the importance of reconciliation as part of the process of becoming married. The resolution of old animosities and resentments is necessary for the process because it opens up channels of communication throughout the family as a whole that will enable support to flow more freely.

The bride and groom are the honored guests at the rehearsal dinner but they are the hosts at the wedding reception. Some couples have chosen to greet people as they come to the wedding ceremony itself. Their first act of hospitality as a married couple, however, is to greet and receive everyone who has celebrated their marriage. As true celebrities, they have the power through the course of the reception to acknowledge and affirm people and relationships simply by their presence and attention. Their second act of hospitality is focused around the table where the cake is cut. Cutting the cake is their first domestic act as a married couple. It is usually carried out with great fanfare. Symbolically, it is also the first time they feed each other. Two people who are now husband and wife do a very private thing in a public place. Through all the celebrations, their natural preoccupation with each other is balanced by attention to the community that has just promised to support them with prayers and other acts of faithfulness.

Pastoral Roles in Pre-wedding Work

There are a number of tasks that need to be accomplished as a couple moves from private expressions of love and commitment to the public declaration at the wedding. The couple will be helped by many people along the way: family, friends, mentors, former lovers, clerks in the store, or strangers in the office of clerk of records. There are also wedding consultants and musicians and informal advisers in the office coffee room to help people get ready to marry. Some couples today have consulted a lawyer in order to write a legal contract that spells out more fully their financial assets and obligations in the event that the marriage fails. As long as most people are married in a church or synagogue, however, there will be a pastoral role. *The aims of pre-wedding pastoral work are to encourage the couple to understand as clearly as possible the lingering impact from their families of origin on becoming married and to plan a wedding that reflects the kind of family they intend to become.*

The Pastor as Friend

Everyone navigating the turbulent waters of wedding preparation needs a friend, and no one needs one more than the bride and groom. People very much in love can still have second thoughts about marrying. Relationships in even the best of families are strained at wedding time. Parents may still be adjusting to their son or daughter's choice of a spouse, or they may be distressed about the wedding plans. In situations where the parents are leaders or generous supporters in the church where the wedding will occur, the pastor may be in a difficult spot if there is conflict between the children marrying and their families. The pastor is often in a position to listen to all sides and mediate the conflict. It is not always easy, however, to be a friend to all sides.

More often than not, what the couple preparing to marry need is a safe haven in the midst of stormy feelings and painful conflict and inevitable confusion. They need someone who is receptive to them without an agenda, someone who is willing to listen nonjudgmentally to their anxieties and doubts and help them discern and plan the kind of wedding *they* want. If the time before the wedding is a period of liminality, even though it is not initiated by a ritual of separation, then those who are marrying need valued companions to walk with them through the transitions in roles and identity that characterize this time.

> At the rehearsal dinner, my daughter was preoccupied with lining up who were going to have their hair done in the morning before the wedding. In retrospect, the hair was incidental. What was primary for Joy was the company of her mother and friends without any distractions. She knew she needed time away from the frenzy that had characterized the weeks before of teaching school and planning her own wedding far from home. The last thing she did before the wedding was to play Scrabble with her grandmother.   (Herbert)

Joy knew the support she needed and was able to find it. Others who are marrying may not be so clear about their needs or so fortunate in resources. The pastor may be a friend for such a couple. Providing nonanxious companions for couples marrying is one contribution that the church can make to enhance the process of becoming married.

The Pastor as Teacher

Catechesis has always been a significant part of religious preparation for marriage. For some, the focus of teaching has been on the religious meaning of marriage. Others have used the time to consider major issues in married life such as money, sexual intimacy, relationships with in-laws, or the need for clear patterns of communication. Because of our emphasis on the significance of the wedding itself, we stress the importance of catechesis in the traditional sense as preparation for liturgy. Education for marriage *is* an important agenda for the church's ministry to couples, but it is more effective in the first years after the wedding. For that reason, we will propose in chapter 5 that the church invest some of the time and energy spent on pre-wedding work in providing ongoing support and guidance for couples in the first years of marriage.

Because it is important to begin with the family stories and personal beliefs and values that a couple bring to the process, preparation for the wedding involves theological reflection. We begin with human experience and move from there to the tradition of faith regarding the significance of marriage. The pastoral task is to help couples move from their own stories and their own values and dreams for their life together, however vaguely religious they might be, to the Christian tradition in order to deepen and expand their vision. To be able to blend liturgical and theological expertise into a process that is truly collaborative is a highly developed pastoral art.

The Pastor as Advocate

From the beginning of planning for the wedding, the pastoral person is an advocate for the other half of a paradox. If one or both of the couple intending to marry need to take steps to enhance their leaving home, the pastor will be an advocate for that individuating process. When a couple is determined to plan an elaborate wedding, the pastor will introduce the idea that something parabolic in the ceremony will be a good reminder of the complexities of married life and the mixture of joy and sadness that will inevitably be present. When one or both of the marital pair insist on preserving continuity with a family of origin in their new relationship, the pastor may become an advocate for letting go of the past as well as holding on to it. When parents do not approve of the kind of wedding their children want, the pastor may need to be an advocate for the children in relation to parents. We are most of all advocates on behalf of the couple and their process of marrying.

The goal of pastoral work with couples before the wedding is to establish a way of being and deciding together that will enhance the process of becoming married. The emphasis here on advocacy should not be confused with tyranny. Nor is it an excuse to violate the sensitivities or traditional expectations of the couple. It is their wedding. Every church will have its nonnegotiable requirements or prohibitions about the ceremony or the participants or the use of the facility. These should be written in a policy statement that is given to a couple when they first initiate contact with the church. The rest is negotiable. Our task is to advocate not only on behalf of the couple but for our understanding of what enhances marrying today. Most of our interventions will occur in unexpected ways. For that reason, being an advocate on behalf of "doing a new thing" in this marriage will depend on having an empathic bond with the couple.

Conclusion

Our emphasis on planning a meaningful wedding in the midst of the parallel processes of leaving and cleaving presumes that the ritual is a transforming moment. A wedding does not make a marriage, but it does make private promises public intentions. It sets forth a vision of being married that becomes a claim from the future to balance the claims from our pasts. It transforms strangers into relatives and gathers a company of friends and relatives (new and old) who promise to support the work of becoming married. The goal of the wedding is to wed. The ceremony will effect the passage to a new social status and initiate a process best if it is a wedding of stories in the parabolic mode.

The approach to *pre-wedding work* we are proposing in this volume presumes *post-wedding* pastoral work as well. The possibility of strengthening marriages is enhanced by greater attention to the struggles of couples in the early years of becoming married. We will turn to a consideration of post-wedding work in a later chapter. It is first necessary to examine more carefully three ordinary aspects of becoming married that in certain circumstances will make the process of pre-wedding work more complex.

4

WHEN THE ORDINARY
IS COMPLICATED

THIS CHAPTER will examine ordinary aspects of becoming married that are made complex by the nature
of the relationship or circumstances at the time of the wedding.
These are issues that are likely to have an immediate and unavoidable impact on the process. We do not regard them as necessarily problematic, but they may be difficult and therefore
require special attention as part of the process of pre-
wedding work. We suggest three: *living with difference, grieving
loss*, and *changing roles*. They provide a beginning framework
for thinking about all the ordinary dimensions of becoming married that are made more complex by the circumstances of a particular relationship.

Becoming Married Means Living with Difference

Every human system must learn how to live with difference and diversity in order to grow and flourish. Diversity is an
inevitable aspect of creation and a sign of God's extravagance.
It is also a consequence of change. Diversity is necessary for
human creativity. Without diversity human beings are not fully
free to be creative because they do not have sufficient options
from which to choose. There are, of course, limits to how much
pluralism creation can bear or how much diversity a human

system can tolerate. But to impose premature or unnecessary limits to difference is a rejection of God's generosity.[1]

Families have different attitudes about diversity. Some families are able to welcome new ideas, or their children's odd friends or unconventional dress, or the changes that occur in the family when mother becomes a bank president. Some families maintain that what appears to be difference is only the outward manifestation of underlying unity. Still others regard difference, whatever it is, as dangerous. Sameness is what is safe. There was a time when a marriage between a German and an Irish Roman Catholic or between a Swedish Lutheran and a Norwegian Lutheran was considered a mixed marriage.

> I came from a family in which difference was discouraged. Most of the time we were expected to agree with my father. One of the fundamental taboos in my pietistic family was listening to popular music that had "pagan rhythms." And so only classical music was allowed to be played on the radio. My wife came from a family in which anyone who liked classical music was pretending. My obvious choice for "music to paint the parsonage by" was Verdi's *Aida.* Not so for Phyllis. It took me a long time to adjust to diversity in musical taste because the choice was tinged with moral judgment. Phyllis added classical music to her repertoire much more quickly. (Herbert)

Musical taste is a *very* simple difference that one would expect to accommodate easily. But when differences in food preferences or political orientation or musical taste are weighted with religious values or family loyalty, accommodating is not an easy matter. It is even more difficult if ordinary diversity is intensified by differences in educational background or economic class or race.

The cultural diversity in this society and others around the globe increases the likelihood of interracial or interfaith or cross-cultural marriages. In some societies, interracial unions are still illegal and marrying outside one's faith tradition is strongly discouraged. Even so, learning how to live with diversity is no longer optional. Because significant age or racial or religious or ethnic or class differences will add to the complexity of becoming married, they require special attention in pre-wedding work.

In order to live with diversity in general, we need to transform our attitude toward the other. Difference need not be dangerous. Nor should it automatically lead to inequality. The ideal may, in fact, be something more like celebrating difference than accommodating it. In celebrating the uniqueness of the other, we are able to see difference as a gift that enriches life rather than as a danger to be avoided or an inconvenience to be ignored. Honoring the uniqueness of the other also diminishes stereotyping. For example, we need to alter the expectation that women will be the primary accommodators in a family because it is their "nature" to sacrifice for the sake of others. Accommodation by everyone is a matter of justice; no one person, whatever the gender, does it all. Learning to accommodate is an absolutely essential ingredient for vital family living.

Celebrating difference also means that reconciling is a necessary component of family living. We will return to this theme in the closing chapter. If we recognize difference, we will need to learn how to practice reconciliation. It is about the prevention of injustice and oppression as well as the mending of broken relationships. In that sense, reconciliation is more than making up after a fight or premature forgiveness. Reconciling as a way of living leads to a new perspective about the differentness of the other. Learning how to practice reconciliation becomes an essential part of becoming married if we intend to honor differences in the family.

Gender is the most obvious difference in any heterosexual union. And it is often overlooked. Although men and women are biologically and psychologically more alike than different, there are nonetheless differences that are inescapable. Whether those differences are from nature or nurture is not what matters; what matters is our attitude toward the uniqueness of our marital partner. *The process of becoming married will be enhanced in our time if we can include an affirmation that women and men are different but equal.*

Our pastoral work with couples before a wedding is informed by the same principles that undergird all pastoral care. We see clearly and listen carefully and advocate fairly because of what we see and hear.[2] The pastor is often in a position to observe how well the couple is able to practice the art of accommodation in relation to each set of parents or each other as they prepare for the wedding. When one partner or one family of origin dominates, or when father's or mother's side of a family is unknown, the pastor becomes an advocate for the other family tradition. Asking about the unknown lineage or giving voice to silent family members is another illustration of "saying the other side" as a mode of pastoral work.

Interfaith Marriage

An interfaith marriage is generally understood as a union in which the religious difference is enough to create distress. Such a definition is broader than the more obvious Protestant–Roman Catholic or Jewish-Christian or Islamic-Christian marriages. It could include the union of a conservative and moderate Lutheran or Episcopalian, bonding between someone who favors the ordination of women or abortion on religious grounds and someone who does not, or marriage between a Mormon or Seventh-day Adventist and a mainline Protestant Christian, or simply between one who is a church member and one who is not. Moreover, even if we marry someone whose beliefs seem compatible with ours, there is no guarantee that he or she will not change. An interfaith marriage is defined by the perception of difference. Therefore it may occur within as well as between major religious groupings.

It has often been said that there is a higher level of marital happiness in religiously homogeneous marriages.[3] People tend to look for spouses with whom they can share tastes and values in the intimacy of family. If, on the other hand, one or both of the spouses are intensely involved in differing religious practice, or if there is an attitude of intolerance toward any kind of difference, or if the couple has unrealistic expectations of what marital love can overcome, religious heterogamy will have a negative effect on the well-being of a marriage. Religious commitment measured by church participation usually declines for both the couple and their children in an interfaith marriage.

The concern over marriages between Protestants and Roman Catholics has been modified some as the differences between them have diminished since the Second Vatican Council. Childbearing and child-rearing practices have become more similar. Even if the differences *are* there, they do not carry the same emotional weight. According to Princeton sociologist Matthijs Kalmijn, "The increase in Protestant/Roman Catholic intermarriage reflects a secularization of *cultural* differences between religious groups. . . . [Moreover] among second-generation European Americans, national origin has become a less important factor in marriage choice while education has become more salient."[4] As a result, marriages are more heterogeneous with respect to religion and homogeneous with respect to education. Couples are less likely to share a common religious tradition and more likely to have achieved a parallel level of education.

Even if religious belief and practice is not a major factor in the lives of the people preparing for a wedding, it is still necessary to explore beliefs and values that may not be thought to be religious but are nonetheless operational. It is an axiom of family therapists that hidden rules have the most power. The same may be said for religiosity. When the religious beliefs and practices are explicit, it is possible, though never easy, to arrive at some accommodation that will enable difference in religion to enhance rather than diminish family living. Beliefs and values that are different and hidden will be a negative factor in family stability because their power is unacknowledged.

What can be learned from one's family of origin about respect for or tolerance of difference will become evident in storytelling around the genogram. It is usually necessary to return to that theme more explicitly when planning the wedding ceremony. How the couple are able to negotiate their way through inevitable religious differences in planning the wedding will be one indication of how they will accommodate difference in their marriage.

> When Randy and I were married, it was still not easy for Roman Catholics and Protestants to marry in our small town. He had been raised Lutheran and I was Roman Catholic. He had also been raised to dominate, and I had been taught that women were the ones who acquiesced. So, even though I was much more active in my church than Randy was, I became a Lutheran and had our children baptized in the Lutheran Church. I took them to church on Sundays while Randy golfed. Whenever he was out of town, however, the children and I would go to Mass at the Catholic church. Randy and I are now separated, and I am very happy to be back in my church. It took me eight years to realize that all of my giving in to Randy had not gotten me anything.   (Darlene)

When the faith differences are significant, even within the same religious tradition, the pastoral pre-wedding work has the delicate task to (1) identify what each individual values, especially hidden or private rituals or beliefs that may be held strongly; (2) enable the partner to hear and acknowledge the religious convictions or fundamental values of the other; and (3) initiate a process by which the couple can begin to negotiate their differences in order to create a context in which their faith can be a sustaining resource rather than a drain on their marriage. Pastors will be particularly helpful at this moment in the process of becoming married if they are able to link their knowledge of religious teaching and function and the rituals of a specific Christian tradition with an awareness of the influence of families of origin in forming the values that are presently held or that may yet emerge.

Interracial Marriage

It was not so long ago that interracial marriages were against the law. In 1967, the Supreme Court overturned miscegenation laws in Virginia and in fifteen other states that made marriage between white persons and black persons a felony. Although interracial marriages have increased slightly in recent time, social acceptance has not. It is still difficult for people to accept a black-white marriage as just another option. When a white woman marries a black man, for example, she may be seen as the enemy of the black family for taking away a marriageable black male. There is also a suspicion that a black man who marries a white woman is confused about his identity and a traitor to his race. The opposition is less but still significant to marriages between white persons and people of Asian or Hispanic origins. At minimum, interracial marriage still causes people to blink and stare. When the one you love and marry is of a different race, marriage is not just a public matter—it is a political one as well.[5]

It is in the public arena that interracial marriages have their greatest difficulty. The wedding is a ceremony by which a couple achieves new social status. It is also a ritual moment in which the community or communities of the couple enter into their marriage by witnessing the public declaration of intent. If the communities from which the individuals come are culturally separated or in conflict, then the couple is isolated in an interracial ghetto in which they must, as a friend of ours once observed, "choose love and disregard the world." Identifying ongoing communities of support in order to include them in the wedding in a tangible way will be especially important for couples whose racial differences have the potential to isolate them.

The racial or ethnic difference between the individuals may be part of the initial attraction. After the wedding, however, the same qualities that were intriguing may become an annoying source of conflict. Life-cycle events may also precipitate a crisis, because they bring to awareness deeper family or ethnic roots otherwise overlooked in the desire to be inclusive. If, however, the rituals that provide the transition through life-cycle crises are celebrated in an inclusive manner, there will be a greater likelihood that people will keep bonding in spite of differences.

The pastor's role in assisting couples to appreciate their differences is like a "culture broker." The first pastoral task may be to help couples and their families set aside the lesson they have learned that *difference is dangerous*. We may also need to help people set aside negative judgments they have made on their own deeply held cultural traditions or ethnic values in order to identify and reclaim them. Resolving issues of ethnic or racial identity in pre-wedding work presumes a multiethnic perspective in which everyone involved is open to honoring values that differ and understanding the value of difference.

Grieving Loss

We have already suggested in a number of ways that grief is a common component of every wedding and the process of becoming married. We mourn for the loss of unquestioned devotion by parents or our freedom as single persons. We mourn for the paths that we choose not to follow or the special relationships that must be reordered when we decide to be a husband or a wife. Most of the time such grief is secondary to the joy of the wedding celebration. In some situations, however, grief may be a more dominant characteristic of the context in which a couple intends the process of becoming married. This is likely to occur in one of three ways: (1) when there is *leftover grief* from a previous marriage that ended because of death or divorce, or from the ending of a significant long-term relationship; (2) when there is *buried grief,* which may in fact be very old; or (3) when a *recent loss* occurs for which there is significant grief. There are also times when the marriage is an experience of profound loss for a sibling, which becomes part of the couple's grief as well.

I was the best man at my twin brother's wedding last year. I was not prepared for the reverberations of that loss in my life. I am preparing to be a Roman Catholic priest. Throughout the wedding I kept thinking about how honored I was to be his best man, standing next to him, holding the rings, giving the first toast. The theme of their marriage was "Today I will marry my best friend." It wasn't until the wedding was over and I returned to my celibate life that I realized all that I had lost: my twin brother, my best friend, *and* my freedom to marry as well. It is a mercy for everyone that my desire to "smash the bride" came after the wedding. What hurt the most was the realization that Christmas, the one stable family ritual in my life, would never be the same again. Fortunately, I like my sister-in-law. So I expect it will be better sooner or later. Right now, however, I am mostly aware of my grief. (Judd)

Judd's story is particularly important because it illustrates again that we do not always know who the primary grievers might be at a wedding. His experience of loss was understandable, and so was the intensity of his grief.

Leftover Grief

In the case of second marriages, people need time between in order to heal the grief and mourn the loss so that it will become possible to honor the memory of the previous relationship. Even when we allow time for grieving to occur, however, there will still be some leftover grief when people embark on a new marriage or relationship. Pre-wedding work with those who have been married before will be developed more extensively in the fourth volume in this series entitled *Promising Again*. We mention it in this context because grief left over from the loss of a previous relationship makes ordinary grief at a wedding more complex for couples marrying again.

Grieving, it is generally agreed, never ends.[6] The pains of loss may diminish in intensity. What was once a painful wound will become, with successful grieving, a poignant and sometimes pleasant memory but not all the longing will disappear. If we have been "one flesh" with another human being in marriage, that emotional bond cannot be severed by either death or divorce. A spouse may die. But people may also choose not to live together any more, get a legal divorce, fall in love, and marry again. Even so, it is not possible to eliminate all memories or emotional investment in one's former partner. In that sense, there is no such thing as divorce.

Then there are the children. The children mourn the loss of a family and regular access to the other parent. For children, the grief lingers longer. Because they may not have the same anger or the feeling of betrayal or terror that necessitates the divorce, it is not as easy to let go of the grief. For some children, even up to the day of the second wedding, they hope that their mother and father will get back together so they can be a family again.

For children and their parent who marries again, planning for a wedding is an exercise in mourning. "Having the patience to tolerate the ambiguity of the situation and allowing each other the space and time for feelings about past relationships is crucial to the process of forming a remarried family."[7]

It is easy to overlook leftover grief. If a first marriage that ended because of death was a good one, there will be memories without regret and the anticipation of new love without fear. And some grief. We would rather not mourn for our first spouse on our second wedding day, but we probably will—a little. If the first marriage ended in a bitter divorce, the scars may take longer to heal, especially if they are covered too soon. Sometimes, when there are no positive memories of the first marriage, we insist there is no grief either. It is important to ask about leftover grief when preparing people for a second or third marriage. In some instances, healing the grief in order to marry again may include being reconciled with negative and painful memories from the past that still linger in the present.

Buried Grief

Sometimes the grief that colors the events surrounding a wedding is old. For example, grandfather had never come to peace over the death of his first wife in childbirth during the first year of their marriage. He did not know how to express the grief, and so he buried it. Every ritual gathering of that family, long after grandfather himself had died, has been colored gray by the shadows of buried grief. Sometimes the grief that is buried by a family for generations is related to a shameful secret. Three generations later, no one knows the secret. What they do know are fixed patterns of interacting in the family that have kept the grief secret but have also inhibited the expression of any intense emotions.

Grief that is not expressed is stored. The reasons for not grieving may be many, but the consequence of stored grief is one: the inability to mourn even ordinary loss. The story of Veronica in chapter 2 is an illustration of the denial of family grief. Her father and stepmother had determined to hide the grief for the loss of their first spouses from their children. In the end, they hid it from themselves as well. In order to deny that grief, they avoided all loss. They formed a family in which leaving home was discouraged and extended adolescent dependency was encouraged. Moreover, it was not possible for Veronica's father to grieve appropriately at the marriage of his only daughter without mourning for her mother. In order to avoid both, he could not be present for the first wedding dance.

The stories of grief are likely to emerge in the genogram. A family history of loss and death is hard to hide. What is less obvious is the family's grieving patterns. It may be necessary to ask about that in doing the genogram or in conversations with the couple. If there is a pattern of burying grief, an important part of pre-wedding work will be to explore the potential impact of that pattern on the new family they are forming. We have found it helpful to ask, "Who will be sad at the wedding?" It may be an aunt who never married. It may be her mother, who married unwisely and unhappily. It may be Grandma, who misses Grandpa. Or it may be the groom, whose father was not invited to the wedding. Or it may be someone whose grief is so secret that no one will know. One can almost assume that every wedding has at least one secret griever.

Burying grief can have significant consequences for growth of a marital bond. If we have to bury our sadness, we usually have to hide other feelings as well. The following story is a striking illustration of the consequence of burying grief two days after the wedding.

> When I met Marvin, I was still in high school and "grounded at home," caring for my invalid father while my mother worked two jobs. Marvin was a wonderful way out. He was older and eager to marry. For most of the time that we dated, we built the house we would live in. Two days after our wedding, Marvin's father died. Obviously, we cut short our honeymoon. From the day of the funeral, however, no one could mention his father's name. When our children were old enough to ask about their grandfather, Marvin said nothing. Neither did I. It was as if he had never lived. When my sister-in-law drowned in a canoe accident, I could not bury my grief anymore. I mourned for her death, for my father's living death as an invalid, and for Marvin's father, whom I hardly knew. For me, it was the beginning of a new life. It was also the beginning of the end of our marriage. You might say that Marvin and I divorced over buried grief.   (Patsy)

Recent Loss

Sometimes the recent death of a parent or a sibling or a grandparent intensifies the ordinary grief of a wedding and may profoundly affect the process of becoming married. The family therapist Evan Imber-Block tells the story of Teresa, who had a difficult time deciding to marry Joey. Joey worked in the same business as her father, made a good living, and was very devoted to her. Like Teresa, Joey was Roman Catholic and Italian.

Joey had been the best friend of Teresa's brother Louie, who had died of cancer a year before. Through the efforts of the therapist, her family (including her father) was able to talk about Louie and mourn his loss and Teresa decided that she did indeed want to marry Joey. At the therapist's suggestion, Teresa and Joey thought about how they would affirm Louie's memory at the wedding. They decided to have a ceremony with the extended family the night before and the best man would mention Louie in his toast to the couple.

Teresa said it was very important to her that people felt free to feel both their sadness and their happiness at her wedding, since she was feeling both and did not want to have to pretend on this most important day. The ceremony on the night before their wedding had been very moving, and had indeed allowed people to experience the full range of emotions without pretense. A favorite aunt had brought a short home movie that showed Teresa, Louie, and Joey during adolescence. Others brought photographs and mementos to frame their remarks. The wedding was beautiful. Everybody missed Louie, but it was ok because they could feel that and say that and not be afraid.[8]

The story is a splendid illustration of the impact of recent loss on planning the wedding. Recent loss is difficult to acknowledge as part of the wedding celebration because it intensifies the simultaneous and conflicting emotions that are present at most weddings. What made this wedding a liberating celebration for the entire family was the determination of Teresa and Joey that everybody would be free to grieve. Other couples have had a special floral bouquet at the wedding in memory of a grandparent or parent who has recently died, and/or have included the recently deceased in the prayers at the end of the ritual.

Instances of recent loss are likely to come to the attention of a pastoral person in a number of ways. They may emerge in the process of doing a genogram as the family's only or most recent experience of loss. They may also become evident because of ambivalence about the wedding that manifests itself in careless planning or confusing postponements. What appears to be reluctance to marry may in fact, as it was with Teresa, be resistance to the inevitable grief of the wedding. Recent loss may also affect a wedding if the couple is determined to do it "just the way Mother would have wanted" (and usually not the way they want), because Mother died just after the engagement and before the planning for the wedding had begun. And if grief for the recent loss is buried wedding joy, it will become a powerful negative force against becoming married and against vital family living. For that reason alone, it is crucial that those who help couples prepare for the wedding pay attention to special grief, old or new, that will intensify the ordinary grief that accompanies the beginning of the marriage adventure.

Changing Roles

Role change is one of the central agendas for couples who are becoming married. If leaving home has gone well, even before one decides to marry, there has already been a change in status in the family that recognizes the freedom and autonomy of an adult son or daughter. However, until people marry, they remain primarily son or daughter despite the new family status. Marriage adds another role and changes the priority. Being married means that one is, or at least ought to be, primarily husband or wife rather than son or daughter. When that role shift is made reluctantly or hardly at all, becoming married may not happen. Ideally, a couple will have time to make the adjustment to the roles of husband and wife before the birth of children adds the parenting role. Having the ability and opportunity to internalize one's role as spouse *before* one becomes a parent is beneficial not only for the family system but for self-definition as well.

Obviously we keep all these roles. What changes at each of these marker moments in the cycles of family living is the significance of the particular role for our self-definition and for our public recognition. The lengthening of the life span and shortening of the child-rearing years has intensified the need for clarity and adaptability about roles in the family. The next volume in this series, *Raising Children,* will examine more closely the transition to the parenting roles. The fourth volume, *Promising Again,* will explore how important it is to recommit to the spousal role when the last child leaves home. Our focus here is on the shift from son to husband or daughter to wife as one's primary role identity.

The transition from daughter or son to wife or husband is difficult if we are reluctant to give up the child role because we would rather be Mommy's boy or Daddy's girl than somebody's wife or husband; or if working our way into the spouse role is complicated by the presence of children, for example, so that being a father or mother has preceded being a husband or wife; or if we have not had good role models for being spouse or parent from our families of origin. Role status is granted as well as claimed. We may have clearly internalized the spouse role even though our parents have not acknowledged our departure from home. Or every community significant to us may have granted the role of wife or husband, whereas we have not as yet claimed it.

In the earlier volume in this series, *Leaving Home,* we noted that the emotional roles we have in our families of origin may keep us from ever leaving and/or determine how we define our place in our new family. If we had the role of the responsible one in our first family, we will frequently replicate that role in a new family unless we choose intentionally to do it differently. We are also likely to follow our families of origin in the ways we fulfill the roles of spouse and parent. It takes hard work to change the role patterns we learn in our first families.

Sometimes circumstances make it difficult for the family or the community to grant *or* for individuals to claim a new family role status. We intend to explore this complex process by examining two situations in which the transition to a new primary-role status is complicated: (1) *When people live together before the wedding*: Ambiguity about roles for those who cohabitate without marriage may make the process of becoming married more complex. (2) *When children from a previous mar-*

riage are present from the beginning of a second marriage: The demands of parenting often leave little time or emotional energy to become married. On the other hand, children may be left to themselves at a difficult emotional transition so that their fathers and mothers can become husbands and wives.

Living Together Before the Wedding

Over the last few decades, there has been an increase in the number of couples living together without or before marriage. There are probably few changes relating to marriage and family living more dramatic than this rapid increase in unmarried cohabitation. The reasons why couples decide to live together vary considerably, ranging from low emotional and physical involvement with minimal commitment to high emotional and physical involvement with maximum commitment. Within that range, there are at least five identifiable patterns:

—a temporary, *casual convenience* with minimum emotional or physical involvement and limited commitment. The motivation may be more economic or protective than romantic.

—an extension of an *affectionate, steady relationship,* which generally includes being sexually intimate. It is likely to continue as long as the couple enjoy being together.

—a *trial marriage* for couples who are contemplating making their relationship permanent and want to test it out. In this sense, living together becomes part of courtship.

—a *temporary alternative to marriage* for people who have determined to marry. They simply live together until it is professionally or economically feasible to marry.

—*a permanent or semipermanent* alternative to marriage. For some people, such as elderly persons, living together permanently is determined by economic factors. For others, this decision may include negative views on the institution of marriage or the desire to keep love alive by avoiding the security of marriage.[9]

While there are theological issues related to nonmarital living together that merit serious consideration, they are not the immediate focus of this essay.[10] The decision to live together has usually been made by the time pre-wedding pastoral conversations begin. Whether the couple are living together may not be something the pastor will know except by asking. If it is known, it may be a barrier to the possibility of a wedding in some religious communities. In some Roman Catholic contexts, the couple must separate before marriage preparation can take place. This book, however, is about enhancing the process of becoming married. We are interested in determining whether and how living together will make it harder or easier to become married.

Partial leaving and cleaving is the issue here. If indeed leaving comes before cleaving, what is the relationship between nonmarital living together and leaving home? In some instances, when the couple relate to their families of origin *as a couple*, and are accepted by those families *as a couple*, living together may challenge families to grant sons and daughters new adult status in the family *as if* they were already married. If the couple are living together in secret or in fundamental opposition to the values of their parents, it may evoke an angry process that makes the work of leaving home more complicated. Or it may be, as in this story of Mark and Janelle, that living together was more like a romantic interlude. Marriage changed things, but not for the better.

> Before we were married we lived together, but we were a long way from Mark's parents. I thought we were pretty independent. We made our own decisions without too much influence from his parents or mine. I figured it would remain that way. After we married, we moved closer to Mark's parents. Now they call him at work all the time and are really a negative influence on our marriage. It seems to me they put more pressure on him than I can, and so they get more of his attention. He tells me that he feels stuck in the middle. He wants to please me but he also

wants to please his parents. Mark is an only child. Before
we married, we talked about putting "us" first. It doesn't
seem like that anymore. I think he worries about their feelings more than mine. I was not prepared for this, because
of the way it was when we lived together.   (Janelle)

In this instance, living together seemed to put the leaving home
agenda "on hold" for Mark. Moreover, as a colleague who
works with young married couples has observed, sexual intimacy outside marriage invites an emotional vulnerability which
is the foundation of love, but it does so without the presence of
a containing environment based on public commitment. Couples may move quickly to physical intimacy as a shortcut to
emotional intimacy and thereby confuse sexual intimacy and
emotional intimacy.

Living together before marriage does not necessarily
function as a liminal period. It is more like being married than
like being in a confusing in-between state of engagement between being single and being married. Moreover, couples usually discover that the wedding changes things more than they
anticipated. Whatever work they did on the relationship while
they were living together needs to be done again as a married
couple. We can hope that what the couple accomplished in
terms of mutual understanding and respect and communication
skills will make it easier to do it again with the new public status of a married couple.

Nonmarital living together shifts the meaning of the wedding. It is more a rite that confirms a relationship that already
exists than a rite of passage *between* living alone or in one's
parental home *and* a relationship in which two people make a
public commitment to become married. It is this potential impact on the process of becoming married itself that has
prompted us to locate this discussion of cohabitation under the
heading of changing roles. People who marry after living together may overlook the work of adjusting to marital roles,
which can only be done after the couple's private bond has been

granted public status and they have been declared to be husband and wife.

Pre-wedding conversations with couples who are already living together should not overlook any of the standard arenas of consideration that we have developed in this volume. There is no guarantee that couples living together have indeed finished the leaving-home agenda. Their experience of living together may have intentionally ignored the marital patterns of either family of origin because they were determined *to do it differently from their parents*. Moreover, while it is possible that cohabiting couples have developed some skills in relating, marriage generally changes things. Being married is more demanding and entails more responsibility and more work than living together. That is not a reason to say people should not live together. It is rather a reminder to those who do pre-wedding work that living together does not eliminate the need for a couple to examine carefully the leaving-home agenda, establish what they intend to include or have already included in their new family from their families of origin, and anticipate the kind of family they want to become.

Second Marriages and Role Complexity

When people marry who have been married before, in most instances they are parents when they marry again. Pre-wedding work in those circumstances must attend carefully to enhancing the process of becoming married without at the same time abdicating parental responsibilities.

When Julie and Riccardo married, each for the second time, neither of them had primary responsibility for the children from their previous marriages. Riccardo's two daughters and Julie's one son were about the same age but of very different temperaments. Nonetheless, because they wanted some weekends just for themselves, they arranged for all their children to come at the same time. Their commitment to each other and to their bonding with

> each other was for a time at the expense of their children. Riccardo and Julie did indeed have complex bonding issues that required a great deal of attention. But all three of the children were being shortchanged on time with their parent. Eventually they worked out a compromise that enabled them to have one weekend per month without children.　　　　　　　　　　　　　　　　(Herbert)

In the concluding chapter of this volume, we will identify sacrifice as a characteristic of being married from a Christian perspective. It becomes a particularly sensitive issue when parents marry for a second time and do not have the freedom they need to bond with a new spouse because of the presence of their children. Unfortunately, the expectation may be, as it was for Julie and Riccardo, that the children should be prepared to give up things so that the mother or father can be happy in a new marriage. In such circumstances, the pastor's role as advocate for commitment to the process of becoming married must be tempered by an awareness that people enter that process with obligations and responsibilities that make it impossible to be single-minded about bonding.

We have already emphasized the reality of grief for children when their parents marry again. Sometimes that grief is intensified by envy because all of a sudden someone else is receiving the attention that the child or children received after the divorce. In such instances, the pastor's task in pre-wedding work will be to advocate for children and their needs while still supporting the couple's desire to bond.

Leaving home may linger as an issue to be addressed in marrying again. There is no assurance that the leaving-home task was completed in the first marriage before a death or a divorce occurred. For some people, in fact, the divorce may be *the* leaving-home moment. In those situations, the wrong person is usually divorced. It may not be necessary, however, to legally divorce one's wife or husband if an emotional separation from one's mother or father can be effected. Sometimes going through a divorce is the occasion for a return to earlier dependency on the home of one's origin and the primacy of the child role. Marrying again means leaving home again, older and more vulnerable.

Understanding the role of the nonparental spouse in the child-rearing tasks is one of the most difficult aspects of remarriage when there are children in the household. Mother's new husband does not automatically become her children's father by marriage. Grandparent roles are equally complex. The parents of the divorced person without custody still hope for access to their grandchildren. One of the consequences of modern marrying and remarrying is that adults clearly outnumber children in the expanded family system. The roles of many of those adults are not yet defined. Also, their access to the children is not fully defined. For that reason alone, pre-wedding *and* post-wedding work with couples who have been married before must take very seriously the unavoidable complexity of family roles.

Conclusion

Throughout this chapter we have lifted up ordinary aspects of becoming married that are made complex by the nature of the relationship or the circumstances surrounding the wedding. There are many other situations that could be explored. Rituals of union that occur without the approval of family or church or society place a special burden on the couple who intend to become married. Pastoral pre-wedding work with couples who begin their life together without approval or in opposition to family or church or society will need to create a context in which the couple feel support and validation of their commitment. Asking the "hard questions" in those situations depends very much on creating an atmosphere of pastoral support.

The pluralism of values in this society makes it almost inevitable that we will be asked to preside at weddings in which the values promoted seem to be in violation of the Christian tradition. Families that spend their life savings to provide a "mythic" wedding for a daughter have not only lost sight of principles of good stewardship—they have also blurred the realities of becoming married. The Christian ideals of hospitality or generosity or justice that the couple selected as a theme may be contradicted by the cost of the wedding or by the fact that children are not invited to the wedding. Good enough pre-wedding work, like good enough marriages, depends on the art of compromise. Weddings are often not how we think they should be. But then neither are marriages.

The focus of this approach to pre-wedding work presumes that the church will find a way to engage newly married couples in ongoing conversations about their process of becoming married. No other social setting can match the church as a place in which people might gather to share the ordinary struggles of married living. The images of "in-service training" or "continuing education in marriage" best describe what is needed to complete the schema of becoming married that we are developing. We turn next, then, to issues facing a couple in the first years of marriage and the necessity of post-wedding pastoral work.

5

GETTING MARRIED
CHANGES THINGS

SCOTT AND I considered ourselves very lucky to
have found each other. We loved being married. Our
first year of marriage seemed like an endless honeymoon.
Then came our first vacation. The fighting began as soon
as we started planning the trip, and things went downhill
from there. We were mildly irritable for the first couple
of days of the vacation and then there was a huge explo-
sion. We said angry things neither of us fully meant.
Both of us wondered if we had made a colossal mistake
in getting married. When we got home, we realized that
the vacation was not the problem. It was us. Neither of us
was as happy with the other as we had thought. I resented
Scott's moods and his distance when he was absorbed in
his work. Scott didn't like my tendency to be messy and
disorganized when I get busy. What confused us both is
that these were things we knew about each other when
we were dating. We had even talked about them. After
the vacation, I wondered how the behavior I accepted before the wedding could have become such a terrible irri-
tant. How could something like that change so much so
soon? (Patti)

The answer to Patti's question is that *getting married
changes things*. And we are usually unprepared for the impact of
those changes. Mild irritants during courtship become annoying

problems later. Traits that were endearing before the wedding lose their charm. The accommodating patterns and the well-intended promises of the liminal time of engagement fade. In their place, the legacies from our families of origin and our own personal histories become the stuff from which we respond to each other in moments of marital intimacy—like planning the first vacation.

Post-wedding Work

Scott and Patti had not deluded themselves. Nor had they made a "colossal mistake." They had begun to encounter, but not yet acknowledge, the loss of illusions that must take place if their love for each other is to deepen. In a conversation with their pastor, Scott and Patti became aware that the families they came from had very different traditions about vacations. Scott's mother was the family travel agent. Every trip was planned well in advance. The rest of the family simply had to show up and be grateful. Patti's family had very little money for vacations. Most of their time was spent with relatives. She had dreamed of going on a trip without worrying about money but she did not know how to plan it. Their arguments were about hidden expectations. These lost expectations are, as Judith Viorst has observed, necessary losses. They are the beginning of lasting, adult love, even though those disappointments are painful when they happen.[1]

We are aware that there are many reasons why two people decide to marry. In marriage we may want a companion who will challenge, delight, support, compete, and play with us. It is also possible that we expect a partner in marriage to provide us with a permanent sense of well-being or to make up for all the personal and developmental injuries we have suffered. We may choose someone who will help us work through the unfinished business from our families of origin.[2] Along with physical attraction and the desire for companionship, our sense of these needs is one of the things that draws us into marriage. The expectations we bring to marriage are often unrealistic. Sometimes the choice of partner is a mistake. Most of the time, however, marriage is about letting go of unrealistic expectations. It is about learning to live with the one we married, who is not quite the one we thought we were marrying.

This chapter is about the hard work of becoming married that follows the wedding. The process has begun before the wedding, but we find that marriage changes things. We are back in *real* time after the liminality of courtship. We make a public declaration to be a "we," while remaining an "I." We initiate a process of becoming married that connects us with our particular family histories. No longer and forevermore, life will not be the same. The wedding makes all this a public reality as well as a private story.

People need to understand their family origins in order to prepare for their wedding and the process that follows. That is the prudent and necessary focus of pre-wedding work. The wedding itself is a parabolic moment in which the couple who are being married ritualize leaving and cleaving, remember their pasts and the promised presence of God, and envision a future toward which they will become. The emphasis on story and symbol in preparation for marriage presupposes a third focus: post-wedding pastoral work. Our intent is to encourage pastors and parishes to *normalize* a process of support for couples becoming married.

The need to support couples becoming married is not new. It is crucial in modern societies, however, because unfettered individualism, intensified by privatizing impulses and institutionalized by the demands of a free-market economy, leads people to be cautious about making the kind of commitment that is necessary to sustain a marriage. The central danger of individualism is that it may result in an "unburdened conception of the self" that is ultimately incapable of forming social bonds.[3] In such a vision, people bond with others only if it furthers their self-interest. Moreover, becoming married is increasingly difficult because people have more choices than they are prepared for. Therefore, we need to be very intentional about assisting couples in the first years to make the kind of bonds that will sustain a life together.

Bonding in the Beginning of Marriage

Becoming married means learning how to live with being separate and becoming connected at the same time. We have described this paradox in a variety of ways throughout the book: one must leave in order to cleave; having a home with a room of one's own; keeping separate and keeping connected; bonding and differentiating. The wedding, which occurs in the midst of parallel processes of leaving and cleaving, is the occasion for shifting the emphasis from differentiating to bonding without overlooking each unique person.

The first elements of bonding have already taken place by the time a couple decide to marry. They have experienced the pleasure of physical intimacy; they have shared dreams for their lives; they have discovered the necessity of making sacrifices for each other; and they may have learned how to fight fairly. They have each begun to internalize the presence of the other and pay attention to the rhythms that keep them close. Preparation for the wedding may be another early bonding opportunity for the couple if they have to weather a storm of parental pressure. The determination to have a better marriage than their parents or to form a family better than the one they came from is another glue that intensifies the process of becoming married.

Bonding is a by-product of what couples do together before and after the wedding. For that reason, we put the phrase in the passive: bonds *are being formed* as the couple shop, plant a garden, make love, paint the bedroom, visit relatives, pray together, or worry about balancing the checkbook. Couples may continue the common work and play that first brought them together. Most couples can remember how struggles in the early years forged a closeness between them. Unfortunately, however, the bonds that hardships foster do not always endure when conditions improve. If the bonding is *only* a by-product of struggle or of common activities, it is likely to diminish when the conditions change that prompted the emotional bond in the first instance.

The couple's bond is shaped by the patterns of intimacy they observed and experienced in their families of origin. If ambivalence, overinvolvement, or isolation were the dominant characteristics of the parental bond, these patterns are likely to be reflected in a newly married couple. If one or both of the marriage partners experienced violence or abuse in their homes of origin, their need for love and their fear of intimacy may not be easily reconciled. We never escape our history; we simply gain greater freedom in dealing with its lingering influence by knowing its content and acknowledging its power.

How Bonding Is Intended

Bonding is also affected by intentional behavior and simple rituals by which couples frame their daily existence. This ritual process begins with betrothal or engagement. It is epitomized in the formal, public declaration of intent to bond at the wedding. That intention is continued in myriad daily patterns by which the couple make an emotional connection. Like leaving home, becoming married happens best when moments in the process are intended.

Couples will develop their own rituals of living together that ensure accessibility and foster familiarity. Rituals of saying hello or goodbye, of playing and fighting, of cooking and eating together and making love become threads in the fabric of a marital bond. In the beginning, these ritualized patterns of relating are important because they represent *conscious* efforts to maintain and foster a connection. Later, as with Kelsey and Manfred, they become part of the meaning and memory of shared life.

> When Kelsey and I were first married, we were very poor. Even so, every time we sat down to a meal, we would light one candle. When the ritual began, it stood for elegance in the midst of poverty. When life became more

comfortable, we continued to light *one* candle at mealtime as a reminder to us of our hard work together; it was a little celebration in the middle of a busy life. When Kelsey was dying, it reminded us of all the wonderful years and the depth of our love. I still light a candle at mealtime.

(Manfred)

Manfred's story is a reminder that keeping rituals alive throughout marriage is a way of maintaining connection. For most couples, bonding rituals or traditions will be unique to their relationship. The subtleties of bonding and the rituals that embody it are endlessly varied. Some couples do not realize the ways in which they are replicating patterns in their parents' marriages. For that reason, it is important for couples to continue the process of exploring the legacy from their families that they began before the wedding.

Not all the ways we bond are positive, however. We may connect with each other around old wounds and present fears or neediness just as easily as we bond around common tasks and shared dreams. The negative consequences of connecting patterns of alcoholism and codependency are self-evident. There are other patterns of bonding, which include abuse or violence or excessive accommodation, that are equally destructive. Continuing to examine the nature of our bonding efforts is one way to ensure that needs and desires outside our awareness do not dominate our becoming married.

When Bonds Are Secret

The expectations that cause the most difficulty early in marriage are the secret ones. These are the hopes that are unspoken and the bargains that are made in silence. They are sometimes so secret or private that they are hidden from ourselves as well as our spouse. We do not know *why* we are unhappy, only *that* our marriage is not what we hoped it would be. Secret contracts are hidden agreements that the couple unconsciously make with each other, based on behavior rather than words. All marriages have them. They are often the basis for choosing a partner.

Their positive function is to maintain the relationship by meeting individual needs. Hidden expectations may become problematic when one partner fails to fulfill her or his end of the contract or when the consequences of fulfilling those expectations are harmful to the individuals or to the marital bond.[4]

> I fell in love with Andy because he was such a strong person. I felt safe when I was with him because he took charge of things. I've always been a little shy and afraid to let people know what I really wanted. In high school I figured there were leaders and there were followers; and I just settled on being a good follower. My dad's a pretty powerful guy, and his word really ruled our household. Mom would fight with him occasionally, but she usually just kept quiet and let him make the decisions. He wasn't mean or anything, he was just always "right." After Andy and I had been married for about a year, I began feeling depressed and pulling away from him. Talking with my mom helped me see that I was angry because Andy was making all the decisions, just like my dad used to. It wasn't so much that he insisted; it was just the pattern we had fallen into. He was the leader and I was the follower. It was the pattern I had agreed to before we married. But now I wanted to change.   (Rheta)

Changing secret contracts is not easy. As long as the inner psychological needs that precipitated the hidden agreement are being met, there is little motivation to change. Both parties must consciously agree to change what had been consented to unconsciously. Rheta's desire to modify her previously hidden expectations of Andy would require his concurrence. If his hopes for the marriage hinge on being in charge, change in their ways of relating could take time. Change is even less likely if the reason for being married to a particular person is equated with an expectation of what that person will do or be.

> Brooks and Sharon had agreed to postpone sexual intercourse until after the wedding. Because of this decision and because of his strong feelings for Sharon, Brooks was

often quiet, not wanting to be romantic or close. Sharon found his quietness very appealing, and so unlike other men she had known. Brooks cried on their wedding night because he was overwhelmed by the depth of his love and passion for Sharon. He had not felt free to demonstrate this before the wedding. Now he showered her with love and affection. He reached for her hand when they walked and held her when they slept. He was a gentle and attentive lover, but Sharon was horrified. This was not the quiet, reticent man she had fallen in love with. Her personal space had been violated. His tears and tenderness embarrassed her. Within an hour after they returned from the honeymoon, Sharon was in the office of the pastor who performed the wedding ceremony, saying she had made a horrible mistake.   (Pastor Post)

Sharon discovered very quickly that her expectations of Brooks and the kind of relationship they might have together were based on a terrible misunderstanding. He was not likely ever to be the kind of person she thought she had married. For Sharon and Brooks, the process of renegotiating a new set of expectations would be like getting ready for marriage all over again.

Becoming married in an age of nonbinding commitments is a complex process. Both autonomy and intimacy are valued. The benefits of a marital bond are measured against the freedom for both women and men to achieve their personal and professional goals. Sometimes the bonds we form are more pragmatic or functional than sexual or affectional. Not every couple will bond in the same way or at the same pace. But bond they must. The process of becoming married depends on mutual and intentional determination to work toward the achievement of a common bond.

Bonds That Are Balanced by Separateness

While bonding is the primary movement in the early stages of becoming married, the need for separateness never changes. The image of a "home with a room of one's own" that we identified in chapter 1 points to the need for balancing intimacy with autonomy in the community of marriage. Attending to the need for separateness is simply honoring the other side of the marital paradox.

The intensity and complexity of the struggle to balance separateness and closeness in the early phase of a marriage will be influenced by several factors. If we come to marriage hungering for but unaccustomed to closeness, we may confuse our spouse by initially wanting all the closeness we can get but then withdrawing to the more familiar stance of distance. If, on the other hand, we have had to fight for independence from our parents, we may continue to seek separateness but never feel quite comfortable being alone. Sometimes the flight from closeness is perceived as necessary for survival. If, however, each individual joining the marriage has established a well-formed self through the process of leaving home, the balance between intimacy and autonomy may be achieved more easily.

Our capacities to be separate and together simultaneously are seldom developed perfectly. Very few people enter adulthood without distortions in their need for autonomy and intimacy and a tendency to protect the area that contains the most discomfort. Moreover, our needs for closeness and separateness change with age and circumstance. In a time of stress associated with a new job or a move to a new community or the enlarging of the family, either partner may want more of the reassurance communicated through closeness. Similarly, when people are feeling stale, bored, or frustrated, they may find the ordinary closeness needs of their partner suffocating. Flexibility, understanding, and good communication skills are the key to responding to the changing needs of each partner.

The hope for marriage is that people are free to move toward increasing degrees of individuation and, paradoxically, toward a greater capacity for intimacy. When the environment of a marriage is experienced by both partners as a trustworthy place, wives and husbands will feel free to discard the false selves that inhibit authenticity. They may also stand up for themselves instead of always accommodating, and they may be able to make choices for themselves as well as for the relationship. Making clear boundaries creates the environment in which the commitment to mutual growth flourishes.

Making a Boundary

We have emphasized throughout this volume that good boundaries make for good bonds. This is certainly so between the marital pair. Being separate and being together is *the* marital paradox. Marriages and families become troubled when one side of that paradox is emphasized at the expense of the other. This same dialectic is equally important for a couple's relationship with each family of origin. One of the ways couples separate from their origins is by sorting out what to include from the legacy each spouse brings from home to their marriage. The couple make a boundary whenever they establish new rituals that modify however slightly whatever they received from their home traditions. Sometimes, however, it is necessary for couples to take more dramatic action when the involvement from a family of origin is particularly meddlesome.

> Alex and I were both in our thirties, successful professionals with a house in the suburbs and money in the bank. But no children. For a while we did not want any. Then when we decided to have children, it didn't happen. All the tests we took showed no medical or physical reason why we could not have children. We tried just everything to become pregnant and eventually we began to think about adoption. My mother was always asking about when we were going to "start our family." When I told her that we were thinking about adoption, she got very upset. That was when Alex and I decided to talk to our pastor. She was very helpful. By means of a genogram, I discovered that my grandmother had two illegitimate children before my mother was born and that my mother had two miscarriages before having me and my brother after long and painful labor. Besides worrying

about fending off my mother's interference, Alex and I had lost the spark in our lovemaking. When we did make love, it was determined by a thermometer which had become for us a symbol of sterility. The pastor suggested that we dig a hole and plant a tree *and* the thermometer in the hole. Alex and I decided on another plan. My mother is a hypochondriac. She never had enough medicine or medical equipment. We decided to give *her* the thermometer for Christmas. Then the symbol of "anxiety about becoming pregnant" would belong to the one who created so much of our anxiety about being pregnant. After that, we started the adoption procedure.   (Stephanie)

The story of Stephanie and Alex illustrates both the ordinary ways in which the boundaries around a couple are invaded (her mother's constant asking about "starting a family") and what a couple can do to make a boundary around their relationship (giving her mother the thermometer). The aim is not to create walls of separation between married children and their parents or siblings. On the contrary, establishing such boundaries is yet another variation of the leaving-home process that continues past the wedding. Couples need to make an invisible separation between their relationship and the families they came from *so that* they are more free to relate to one another in life-enhancing ways.

Commitment to Growth

The process of becoming married includes a commitment to create an environment in which growth and change are nurtured. The universal truth that human beings need one another to grow is most specifically true for marriage. Loving another person means learning to support the process by which that person is able to become everything she or he might become. Quite often, that is a scary process. "If she becomes less dependent on me, will I continue to be important in her life?" "If he pursues his real dream to be an artist, will I ever have the financial security that I never had as a child?" There are no guarantees in marriage. If, however, there is no freedom for individuals to grow within a marriage, either they and the marriage will stagnate *or* they will find a context in which to grow outside the marital bond.

> It had been bubbling inside me for a while, but when our daughter, Jessica, was four years old and ready to be in nursery school at least part of the day, I began to admit to myself that I was no longer content with the role of wife and mother. When Matt and I were married, he already had a responsible position and made an excellent salary, so I was pretty content to stay home and raise a family. When I first brought up the idea of returning to school, Matt was amused by the idea. Later he got angry and made some pretty nasty remarks. He told me that a wife in school and a kid in day care was not what he had in mind when he married me. I was hurt and pretty intimidated at first, but somehow I found the courage to pursue the idea. I loved Matt and our daughter and our life together, but I loved math too. We were pretty far apart and scared when we went to see our pastor.   (Karen)

The challenge that Matt and Karen faced was complicated but not atypical. Matt's response was understandable. Karen had changed the marriage contract to which they had subscribed; namely, that Matt would earn a good living and Karen would stay home and tend the family. Matt was surprised and confused by the strength of his reaction. It took a lot of talking between themselves and with their pastor before they were able to agree on the course Karen had chosen. Each compromised. Karen began her studies part time. Matt picked up more of the parenting responsibilities and turned down a promotion that would have moved them to another city. That decision in particular was not an easy one for Matt to make. Eventually, however, Matt realized that Karen's decision had saved him from doing exactly what his father had done, becoming addicted to his job and unavailable to his family.

Creating an environment in marriage in which the growth of husbands and wives is supported equally is a demanding but inescapable agenda for our time. It may require a reexamination of traditional living patterns. We may need to reconsider our assumptions about parenting. Also, the demands of a free-market economy for individual mobility will need to be modified. The working assumption must be that wives and husbands are both life planners and decision makers. Everyone has an equal say, even when the needs or possibilities are not equal. Marital decisions in the future will require at least two datebooks and lots of willingness to accommodate.

Elements in Fashioning a Marital Bond

The development of a workable balance between separateness and connectedness is the first and primary task of becoming married. The ideal is to fashion an environment in which it is possible to be autonomous in community. There are a number of elements of a marital bond, however, that couples must develop during the early years if the marriage is to become a community of wholeness and growth. They are all related to the core processes of connecting and separating, but each is specific enough to warrant attention. We mention four: *fostering intimacy, sharing power, communicating clearly,* and *recognizing the other.*

Fostering Intimacy

Sexual attraction and satisfying physical intimacy bring people together and effect early bonding. People who are in love are glad to be together, look at one another, touch each other. The romance of courtship does not and certainly should not end with the wedding or honeymoon. The longing for physical intimacy is an important dimension of being married, but it is rarely the most complicated. The ability to deepen the emotional intimacy begun in courtship is often more troublesome for newly married couples. By emotional intimacy we mean the capacity to disclose oneself and become vulnerable to another person in more than a physical way.

> I remember waking up one morning and realizing how utterly dependent I had become on Diane's presence next to me in bed. In the four years of our marriage, I had come to love and respect her in a way that I had only glimpsed when we married. It was a little scary to realize how important she had become to me and how thin my pretense of total self-reliance had become. I was immensely grateful for the grace that had come to us through the very ordinary process of becoming married. (Robert)

The ability to be vulnerable is a gift not equally given. Despite the progress men are making, women remain more comfortable and competent in identifying and expressing emotions. Men often mistake physical intimacy for emotional intimacy and are confused when their wives complain of the distance between them even though they make love frequently.

Being vulnerable in order to foster emotional intimacy involves several things. First of all, it presumes *self-awareness*. The thoughts and emotions that determine how we live are usually several levels below polite social conversation. The hopes and fears, joys and sorrows, certainty and confusion that are the stuff of everyday life are rarely the topics of social conversation. Nor should they be. Not everyone can be trusted with the intimate details of our lives, and not everyone is interested. However, each marital partner needs to know what the other feels and what the other thinks. Too often, communication between husbands and wives in marriage depends on one person guessing what the other is thinking or feeling.

If awareness is the first challenge, *acceptance* is the second. When we reveal our deepest fears and dreams and our secret impulses to our marital partner, the fear is that they may not be accepted. It is a risk worth taking, however, because if we can name our deepest fears or desires to someone we trust, we are less likely to act on them. When another person recognizes and accepts our most personal dreams and hidden fears, it is an experience of grace. At the beginning of a marriage, those thoughts and feelings often have to do with our sexuality. Marital intimacy will be strengthened if intimate conversations between men and women are characterized by circuits of recognition. We will return to the theme of recognition later.

Being emotionally intimate in marriage takes *courage.* That is the third element. Few of us relish the notion of revealing our less than noble selves to someone important to us who might be disappointed in or, worse, repelled by what we say. Some fear that exposing a vulnerability may be used against us in a fight. It takes courage to tell a spouse of a vocational failure or an embarrassing fear or a lingering fantasy. The irony is, of course, that in most relationships such a disclosure ushers in understanding rather than judgment. Nothing promotes greater intimacy than the relief of a burden no longer carried alone and the deepening of trust that comes when our hidden self is recognized and accepted by the one we love.

> When we were first married, I was grateful that Steve was more sexually experienced than I was. His comfort and confidence when we made love encouraged me to experiment more with our lovemaking and to get more enjoyment for myself. Our sexual relationship was not the most important factor in our decision to get married, but, as I look back, it was a strong one. We developed the other aspects of our relationship as we got to know each other, so I felt pretty good about our decision to marry. What most surprised me after we got married was the jealousy I felt about the other relationships Steve had had before we met. I even began to wonder if he would lose interest in me as he did with former girlfriends. And for quite a while that really shut me down . . . until I worked up the courage to tell him how I felt. I was embarrassed about bringing it up, but he had already figured something was wrong anyway; we hadn't made love for several weeks. He was confused at first by my feelings, but we eventually talked it out, and I came to realize how much my family's discomfort with closeness and my fear of guys in high school had affected me. Surprisingly, the whole thing brought us closer together. (Colleen)

Physical intimacy is the delightful companion of emotional intimacy; but sex becomes distorted and ultimately disappointing when it is cut off from emotional closeness. While sexual attraction may be what draws people together, it is rarely what keeps them together. The first years of a committed relationship are sometimes described as a sexual dance in which the partners are trying to get in step with each other, determining who will lead and who will follow and in what sequence. If partners are respectful of each other, they will develop a sexual dance that honors the particularity of each personality involved and the complexity of their life together. Without such respect and open communication between husbands and wives, fears and resentments are likely to build up that will eventually restrict the sexual pleasure that may have characterized the early stages of the relationship. *The qualities that will help a couple develop a fulfilling sexual life are the same as those which will nurture the relationship itself: mutual respect, trust, openness, and flexibility.*

Sharing Power

Just as there is a sexual dance going on in the early years of marriage, there is also a dance related to power. The struggle to share power goes beyond the traditional areas of sexuality and money. It pervades almost every aspect of marital life together, involving such issues as who does the housework, who cares for the children, whose family tradition predominates, how leisure time is organized, how decisions are made, or who writes the Christmas letter. Sharing power, like making decisions and distributing responsibilities, is an especially important agenda for people who marry after living on their own for a time.

The growing practice of preparing a financial contract prior to the wedding suggests something of the complexity of marriage today. When women and men are both capable of financial independence, merging assets is a profound experience of sharing power. Even when couples intend to avoid conflict over money, it will still occur. No two people have the same configuration of needs related to money. There is probably no aspect of life where family patterns influence us more. Maxims like "A penny saved is a penny earned" or "It only costs a little more to go first class" suggest profoundly different attitudes toward money from our families of origin. People who are financially secure may drive a marital partner to distraction by spending their leisure time shopping for the best bargains. It is often problematic for couples who may otherwise think about themselves as liberated if the wife earns more money than her husband. Having money is having power. Learning how to balance a joint checking account is a beneficial lesson in sharing power. Learning how to live within a budget when money is tight is a necessary lesson in shared power.

Cleanliness and order and the organization of life are often surprisingly important aspects of ourselves. There is merit in these traits in and of themselves, but they are also ready repositories for unresolved control needs. Adolescents use this arena to establish their tenuous sense of independence. Children can drive their parents to distraction with a jacket carefully dropped in an otherwise immaculate hallway. The sloppiest children at home, however, frequently become paragons of order and organization when they marry and begin raising their own children. The most common subject of anecdotes about marital conflict used to be the toothpaste tube. It has probably been replaced by a more obvious symbol of power: the TV channel changer.

> When we were married, we were pretty clear that Delbert was going to be the main source of financial support for our family and that I was going to raise our children. If we could afford it, we wanted a traditional marriage. When Jenny, our first child, was born, the level of organization and neatness in the house dropped several notches. I began to notice that when Delbert came home at night, he would go through a flurry of cleaning up before he paid much attention to me or Jenny. I resented the unspoken judgment and the implication that cleanliness was more important to Delbert than we were. When I

was finally able to express my hurt and anger, Delbert was only half aware of what he was doing. He was working at the time in a very chaotic office, and he never left the job feeling that his area of responsibility was under control. So he came home and ran around cleaning up so he could feel some control in his life. As Delbert talked more about his dissatisfaction at work, his need to "clean house" began to diminish. He was still more intent on putting things away than I was, but we learned to laugh at his tidiness impulses and keep them from interfering with our relationship. (Helene)

Time is another arena for power struggles, and, like money, sex, and cleanliness, its management involves issues shaped by the family of origin. We have all rejected or internalized or in some other way modified maxims from our origins about the perception of time and the value of punctuality. These differences are difficult to negotiate in marriage. The partner who is anxious about pleasing others will chafe at the spouse who delays getting ready for a dinner engagement. Likewise the perpetual dawdler who may be expressing unresolved conflicts about autonomy will experience the impatience of a spouse as an attempt to control. On the other hand, when both spouses work at demanding jobs, time manages the relationship. It is difficult to share power when there is no time to negotiate. Couples need to trust that power, like work and privilege and responsibility, will balance out in the long haul.

Power is a great gift in marriage if it is shared. When everyone is empowered, love flows more freely and conflicts are settled more quickly. When the power is out of balance, then decisions about who initiates sex, what money is spent for, how clean the bathrooms are, which relative to visit at Christmas, or the use of leisure time are the occasion for heavily weighted conflict. Even under the most positive circumstances, sharing power in marriage is determined by many factors: by the individual's needs and fears, by values from our families of origin, by our understanding of gendered roles, and by the particular cultures within which we have been raised.

Communicating Clearly

Nothing tests the process of becoming married more quickly and effectively than how we communicate in marriage. Couples who describe their marriage as positive and fulfilling often attribute the success to their ability to talk things out. No matter how difficult or painful the subject, they report that their determination to keep talking and listening to each other is what has deepened and solidified their marital bond. When a couple seek help for their relationship, they will often describe their difficulty as a problem of communication. "We just don't seem able to talk to each other anymore," they say. That usually means someone is not listening.

The most important thing to anticipate in the early stages of becoming married is that the openness a couple felt before the wedding does not always remain constant. Living together as wife and husband evokes surprising and sometimes unsettling dimensions of our person. Beyond the uniqueness of each personality, there are social, cultural, and gender differences that affect the way people learn to talk to each other.[5] Moreover, every family has its own history and patterns of communication that are part of the legacy one brings to a marriage. Who talked with whom? About what? What could be talked about and what couldn't? These family histories contribute to how each of us learns to handle fear, shame, guilt, anger, joy, sorrow, success, and failure. The variables are infinite, and each affects our ability to communicate.

This text cannot be a primer on communication. There are ample resources that explore the subject in depth.[6] Yet there are some fundamental guidelines that are simple to describe even though they are difficult to carry out. Effective communication, particularly about conflicted or emotionally laden issues, consists of at least five things: It is direct; it begins with "I"; it incorporates appropriate feeling and rationality; it is timely; and it is well-intentioned.

Good communication is direct. So much unhappiness is spawned because couples fear to say directly what concerns them. Indirect communication adds another layer of conflict when it becomes the avenue for expressing the concern. Silence and withdrawal and general irritability are among the patterns of indirect communication we bring to marriage from our families of origin. Direct communication takes courage and enough trust in ourselves and the relationship to risk saying what matters to us.

Good communication begins with "I." When there is conflict, sentences that begin with "you" are usually accusatory and blaming, and they elicit defensiveness. Statements like "You are so messy" or "You are more interested in your stupid job than you are in me" do not foster further conversation. Sentences that begin with an "I" may seem awkward at first, but they are not as likely to evoke defensiveness or a counterattack and may even invite truth-telling and reconciliation.

Good communication incorporates both rationality and feeling. Feelings are an important dimension of communication, but they are not its exclusive commerce. There is a place for thought and for rational analysis when it is not just a defensive cover for the feelings that underlie it. When women talk only with feelings and men only with thoughts (the stereotypes of women's and men's talk), it continues to make conversations between women and men unsatisfying. Effective communication in marriage depends on a balance between thinking and feeling *and* the freedom for both husbands and wives to communicate both ways.

Good communication is timely. It is common that serious conversations about this or that aspect of marital life together begin at inconvenient times. When a spouse is already late for school or has just walked in the door after a long day at work, it is not the best time to initiate an intense conversation about feeling ignored. When a spouse is hurrying to prepare for guests to arrive, it is not the time to make some observations about entertaining too much. There are obviously some times that are better than others, but sometimes the only good time to have *the conversation* is when it begins. Whatever time is finally chosen to engage a difficult issue, it takes courage to communicate.

Good communication is well-intended. That sounds obvious, but it is probably the most significant *and* the most forgotten factor. Love takes on a very concrete form when loving intention is present. Many of the mistakes that couples make in their efforts to communicate with each other—both omissions and commissions—can be forgiven when the intent is benign. No amount of communication skills makes up for lack of loving intent. First Corinthians 13 has it right. If love is not present, all our talk is just a lot of irritating noise. But love that is kind and truthful and upbuilding does not come easily. It is a gift of grace when we find it.

Recognizing the Other

The freedom to grow and develop one's gifts within the bonds of marriage will be enhanced by the willingness of each partner to recognize that growth and those gifts in the other. In *The Bonds of Love*, Jessica Benjamin links self-assertion with mutual recognition if two people are to meet as sovereign equals. "Assertion and recognition constitute the poles of a delicate balance."[7] We never outgrow the need for recognition that begins in the interaction between a newborn child and its mother.

> Recognition is that response from the other which makes meaningful the feelings, intentions, and actions of the self. It allows the self to realize its agency and authorship in a tangible way. But such recognition can only come from an other whom we, in turn, recognize as a person in his or her own right.[8]

In order to experience recognition in the fullest sense, "you" who are "mine," whom I have internalized as part of "myself," are also different, other, even a stranger to me. Marriages that endure and flourish have achieved a kind of mutual recognition between husband and wife that honors the spouse as a separate and unique subject. If a marital bond is characterized by dominating the other or making the other an object, recognition in the sense that Benjamin means it is not likely. If, however, both wife and husband are equal subjects in the marriage, if their relationship is marked by mutual respect rather than domination, then it will be possible to fulfill every individual's longing for recognition.

> The vision of recognition between equal subjects gives rise to a new logic—the logic of paradox, of sustaining the tension between contradictory forces. Perhaps the most fateful paradox is the one posed by our simultaneous need for recognition and independence: that the other subject is outside our control and yet we need him.[9]

Recognizing the other is a prerequisite for empathy. It is a way of understanding that begins with the other's uniqueness. To be empathic is to understand the distinctive world of one's wife or husband on the other's terms. To be empathic is to imagine a world different from one's own but equally valid. To be empathic is to respond to the emotions of another without taking responsibility for them or eliminating them. Being understood is more important than being right. And recognizing the other is preliminary to understanding in an empathic mode. Relationships that endure and grow depend on recognizing and understanding the other.

Jessica Benjamin's thoughts are important here because understanding with her the paradox of equal subjects in relationship deepens the process of becoming married. *There is no theme more necessary for a vital marriage than this need for recognition.* Each partner may have a fully individuated self, but recognition of that uniqueness by the other is necessary for the marriage to work. We have already noted in chapter 4 the importance of honoring difference. But even respect for difference does not guarantee the end of domination. The first step in untangling the bonds that stifle is to embrace this paradox of recognition and independence. Marriage, from that perspective, will be characterized by circuits of recognition rather than shackles of domination.

Leavening the Process of Becoming Married

The communities that gather to witness the beginning of a marriage pledge to do all in their power "to uphold these two persons in their marriage." It is a promise often ignored. Sometimes we do not keep the promise because couples move to a new town or form new social networks in the same town. Sometimes we keep our distance from the newly married in order to honor their privacy or to insist that, whatever the struggle, they need to work it out for themselves. Couples who intend to establish a committed relationship seek to incarnate a fundamental truth: human beings are meant for community.

Religious communities are in a unique position to provide support and sustenance for couples becoming married. No other institution has ordinary access to people at significant moments in the life cycle. Moreover, whenever a religious community gathers, there are a variety of examples of being and becoming married for young couples to observe and interact with. *Because of the value religious communities place on the sanctity of the home, they have a special responsibility to leaven the process of becoming married.* Leaven is a relatively small substance that transforms the structure and substance of the whole. There are three ways by which religious communities might enhance the process: *pastoral conversation, ongoing education,* and *formation for faithful family living.*

Pastoral Conversation

The process of becoming married is just beginning on the wedding day. This proposal for ministry with those becoming married presupposes the need for education and reflection after the wedding. It is, we believe, an even more productive time than before the wedding to focus on the particular struggles of a particular couple to form a particular marital bond. Therefore, the pastoral conversation that was initiated with the premarital exploration of families of origin needs to be continued at various points after the wedding. This can be done most effectively by scheduling in advance periodic visits during the first years after the wedding. Inviting the couple to contact a pastor if they have some difficulties puts them in the awkward position of admitting that already in the marriage all is not well. It is better to make plans for such meetings during the pre-wedding preparation, on the assumption that every couple will have some struggle in the process of marrying.

When religious communities have established common bonds and a trustworthy mutual support, there is a natural process by which people in community talk with one another, tell their stories, and thereby empower themselves to manage conflict, heal divisions, and restore hope. Professional marriage counseling is necessary if the marital conflict is serious. Newly married couples, however, may be helped by their religious community through spontaneous conversations that invite the couple to describe their struggles in becoming married. Before the wedding, the announcement of engagement is an invitation for public conversation about marriage. Communities of faith are an ideal place for these conversations to take place.

It is not enough, however, to leave these conversations just to the general community. Although smaller groups of people do not supplant the contributions of the larger community, gathering people who share a common life experience such as becoming married or having the first child or losing a parent accomplishes several things. It breaks down isolation, normalizes the struggles, and multiplies the possibilities for addressing the situation. For support groups to become truly leavening conversations, there needs to be an acceptance of people's experience with no effort to minimize or fix it, a realistic search for new ways to face the challenges, and support that empowers rather than depletes.

Ongoing Education

Religious communities have become very creative in designing educational programs that do more than impart information. Sermons, workshops, seminars, and retreats are all avenues for helping couples with some of the issues in becoming married that have been identified in this volume: honoring differences, changing roles, communicating clearly, sharing power, and recognizing the other.

There has been less creativity in providing the kind of education that takes place through *mentoring*. Mentoring includes imparting information, but it is "incarnational" information, communicated through personal presence and the stories people tell about themselves. It also implies a personal commitment to another person. When married couples have lived together long enough to know how painful and rewarding the process of becoming married can be, they can be a valuable resource for mentoring others at the beginning of the process. The simple truth is that we need to learn from those who have gone before, and the church is a natural community in which that might happen. Selecting couples for this ministry of mentoring must be done carefully.

> Otto and Irene Krueger were about to celebrate their fiftieth wedding anniversary when we first met them. Jasmine and I had been married for six months and we had just had our first major fight. The young couples group in the church was asked to prepare the refreshments for our congregation's celebration of the Kruegers' fifty years of marriage. We were deeply moved by the liturgy that celebrated their relationship, but what really got to Jasmine and me were the stories they told about their marriage. They told about the sorrow they experienced when they lost their second child and how they almost separated when their kids left home. And then they talked about the deep companionship they enjoy now. (Bill)

Formation for Faithful Family Living

Linking the stories of families of origin and the new family in process with the stories of faith is an ongoing religious agenda. The church has the unique gift of being able to join the meaning of the present moment with meaning woven through a historic community of faith. People are formed for faithful family living through the weekly rituals that sustain a religious community. Our faith for family living is also formed by mentors and others like Otto and Irene Krueger, who testify to the presence of God in their experience of family living.

Human beings are meaning-making creatures, and ritual is one of the ways we create and communicate that meaning. In the early years of marriage, couples are usually still sorting out the rituals they bring from their family of origin. They are also making up their own unique rituals as the marriage is forming. From the most informal and homely to the most formal and elegant, those rituals are the way we frame the important moments of our lives. Rituals are what anchor us in the deeper values and commitments that give society its substance. What couples need to discover are ways of being formed for faithfulness in marriage that will link their journey to the stories of faith and rituals from their religious traditions. We turn to that agenda next.

6

A Covenant of
Abiding Seriousness

∇ THE PROCESS of becoming married does not occur in a
vacuum, but in a context that includes what we believe about marriage. The content of those beliefs in turn shapes
the process. Becoming married occurs within a framework of established religious teachings and social traditions about the
meaning of marriage. It is also a process shaped by implicit expectations and beliefs about what marriage means that are drawn
from our experience and from the common culture. Our intention
in this concluding chapter is twofold: to examine the connection
between the content of Christian beliefs about marriage and the
process of becoming married; and to propose a way of being
married that reflects the tradition of faithful Christian living.

The Diversity of Beliefs About Marriage and Family Living

There are two questions that we need to ask in order to
understand the relationship between content and process: How
do traditional theological understandings of marriage affect becoming married? What are themes from the tradition that might
become a couple's vision for marriage and family living in
Christian perspective? The first question asks about a theology
of marriage; the second is about a theology *for* marriage. It is
important for people planning to marry to ask both questions in

order to make explicit unspoken assumptions about their meaning of marriage and in order to identify a vision of life together that might become a goal for becoming married.

Articulating underlying beliefs and expectations of marriage is necessary in our time for three reasons: (1) There are powerful forces in the wider culture that are likely to determine the way people think about becoming and being married unless couples are able to utilize their faith as a resource for understanding the meaning of marriage. (2) Because people experience a growing freedom in relation to traditional religious expectations, there is a widening gap between official church teachings and the operational theologies by which people live. For that reason, even people who come from the same faith tradition or denomination may believe different things about marriage. (3) People more frequently marry outside their racial or cultural or religious heritage than in former times. Different beliefs about marriage in the same relationship are likely to be the norm rather than the exception. Moreover, because we are often dislodged from our cultural and religious roots, there is less reinforcement from our social context for the beliefs we have been taught and may still hold in tentative ways.

Everyone has some understanding, however vague, of the meaning or purpose of marriage. That understanding, even if unspoken, creates the framework by which people determine gender roles, establish boundaries between the family and the outside world, make and keep friends, and decide how and for what money is spent. Those assumptions become an operational theology when the authority of God or the church is invoked in support of a particular view of life. The growing secularism and the corresponding decline of traditional forms of authority mean that the theologies by which people live have less and less to do with deeply held traditional values or official church teaching.

In addition to these particular and often highly personal operational theologies, there are differences among Christian churches regarding the meaning of marriage. In the Roman Catholic tradition, marriage is a "symbol and sacrament of love resulting from the covenant between Christ and his Church."[1] Similarly, Orthodox theology regards marriage "as a form of human community in service to the Church and the Kingdom of God."[2] When husband and wife become one flesh in marriage, they are an ecclesial reality that expresses Christ's love to the church. The Protestant perspective varies widely, but it generally connects marriage with God's creative activity. "As a natural experience it can be a metaphor *for* faith in that it gives us vivid images for speaking about God's action."[3] Because it is common to all humanity, marriage is first of all a civil rather than an ecclesial concern.

Themes for a Theology of Marriage

As long as people continued to marry within their faith groups, fundamental theological differences regarding the meaning of marriage would not occur within a particular relationship. There would be cultural variations if a Swedish Lutheran married a German Lutheran, but the religious understanding of marriage would be similar. If, however, a Polish Roman Catholic from Chicago marries a Southern Baptist from Kentucky, there will be both cultural and religious differences. The increasing frequency with which people marry across different church traditions within Christianity and even across major faith traditions has contributed to a blurring of the distinctive theological perspectives on marriage.

When this shift away from denominational particularity either in choosing a mate or in understanding marriage is linked to increasing secularism, it is not surprising that people who come to a minister to prepare to marry may be quite vague about what they believe is the religious significance of marriage. Nico ter Linden, the pastor of the Westerkirk in Amsterdam, does not take faith for granted when he begins the conversation with a couple. Often, he has observed, one of the couple may not even consider himself or herself a believer.[4] For that reason, he begins with the images or stories of marriage that the couple may have drawn from the common culture as well as their faith tradition.

Because the interpretation of marriage is less fixed to a particular Christian tradition, it becomes even more important to identify what the various Christian traditions hold in common. We suggest five themes that form the core content of a theology *of* marriage: *sacramentality, indissolubility, intentionality, fidelity*, and *covenant*. It is not our intent to do a comparative analysis of these themes, but rather to explore the implications of each of these themes for the process of becoming married. Our aim is to examine whether or how our theologies of marriage make it harder or easier to become married.

Marriage as Promise and Sign of God's Grace

It is commonly held that marriage is instituted by God. The story of Jesus at the wedding at Cana is used frequently in the wedding ritual itself to remind us that God is present to bless the couple and their marriage with an abundance of grace. Although not every Christian tradition defines marriage as a sacrament, it is generally regarded as an institution that God intends and promises to sustain. Marriage is a "holy estate" or a "sacred calling" even when it is understood as a civil institution belonging to the realm of creation rather than redemption. The belief that God intends marriage is a promise that sustains our fragile determination to effect a marital bond.

Those traditions that regard marriage as a sacrament see it as a sign of the love between Christ and his church. Christian marriage is understood to be a prophetic symbol and sacrament of the community of love resulting from the covenant between Christ and his church. In his work *Marriage: Human Reality and Saving Mystery*, the Dutch Roman Catholic theologian Edward Schillebeeckx has shown how the biblical image of covenant is expressed in language taken *from* the experience of human love which in turn becomes the standard *for* human married love. God's covenant with humankind is like marriage, and human marriage is like God's covenant.[5] It is a promise not broken.

If becoming married happens over time, then the wedding is more than an event that establishes a new status. It is, as we have said in a number of ways, a moment in a much longer process. Like baptism, the ritual of marriage is a moment that must be complemented by a process that itself becomes sacramental.

James and Evelyn Whitehead have developed this idea in their book on *Marrying Well* in the following way:

> The sacrament of marriage cannot be understood in terms of a single ritual which magically transforms us from two into one forever. The sacramental celebration of marriage in the rites and ceremonies of the Christian Church must be the celebration of a process already well under way and of a process which has still some considerable way to go.[6]

We concur. We also agree with their insistence that the process of becoming married needs the sustaining presence of a community of faith that embodies concretely the promise that God will not abandon us in our struggle to be faithful in marriage.

There is a sense in which the understanding of marriage as a sign and symbol of God's grace is both burden and blessing. It may be experienced as burden if being a sign of God's love adds another responsibility to an already difficult task. Marriage becomes a sacrament from this perspective insofar as a couple are able to establish for themselves an "unbreakable covenant fidelity." In that sense, being in a sacramental marriage is a contingent reality. Expecting marriage to be a sign of God's love may be burdensome for a couple if just staying in the relationship is very hard work.

The idea of marriage as sacrament is a blessing insofar as it is a reminder to the couple that their life together is undergirded by the promise of God's grace and the sustaining love of a community of faith. Again the Whiteheads have said it well. "We know, sometimes with frightening clarity, that this intricate and often fragile figure of our life together depends altogether on us, and altogether on more than us. It is our responsibility, and yet we receive it as gift."[7] The idea of marriage as a sacramental reality is a useful reminder that our life together is our responsibility; it is something for which we must work hard *and* a gracious gift of love that we discover in the midst of that hard work.

Till Death Us Do Part

We begin marriage with the expectation that it will last forever. But many marriages do not. Sometimes our expectations of permanence are shattered by the premature death of a spouse. Other times, what begins with the promise to be together forever ends with subpoenas or restraining orders from the court or a judge's decree, rather than death. Divorce, whenever it occurs and for whatever reason, is a tragic ending of what is usually a happy beginning. Men and women mourn the loss of a dream, even though there may have been little love and no affection long before there was a divorce. Friends and family take sides and the damage to the wider family is not easily repaired. Most of all, the children suffer.

Divorce is tragic but it is understandable. To make a promise to be married to someone forever when death was likely to sever the bond after ten to fifteen years was one thing; to promise at age twenty-five to be married for sixty years is almost incomprehensible. The expanded life span of individuals, and so potentially of a marriage, does not diminish the necessity of thinking about marrying for life but it does make commitment for a lifetime a more complex promise. It takes boundless love, considerable patience, probably a little stubbornness, and the abundance of God's grace for a marriage to last that long. In the fourth volume of this series, entitled *Promising Again*, we will consider recommitment as a necessary condition for staying married until death parts us.

There is a point of view that is fashionable from time to time that eschews marriage of any kind because the permanence of a marital relationship endangers the existential vitality of the love of partners for each other. Choosing every day anew for the one we love, according to this perspective, keeps the commitment from going stale. It also keeps the options open. An image of marriage as forever may lead to complacency by one partner or the other. It is much too easy to become preoccupied with work or children or personal growth and take the marriage for granted. When we take love for granted, we do not always work to keep it alive.

People may also avoid the work of becoming married if they begin with an expectation that the relationship is *not* permanent. We are less likely to invest in activities or relationships that are temporary or even possibly temporary. As demands on our time become more and more complex, people will invest themselves where they expect some return. If the marriage is not perceived as having any long-term benefit, there is diminished investment in the process, which in turn increases the likelihood that a marriage will end long before death parts the couple. However, if we begin the process of becoming married with the assumption that the marital bond is for life, that it will outlast our work relationships and our friends at the club, then it is worth investing in even without religious motivation.

Whenever two people fall in love, the bond is forever. In that sense, permanence is inevitable. When bonding occurs, emotional divorce is not possible. We may fall out of love or end a marriage relationship, but we cannot sever those ties altogether. The theological significance of permanence is a mirror of the psychological reality that bonds are forever. This is an important perspective to keep in view, particularly when people marry for a second time. It is equally necessary for people marrying for the first time to understand that the bonds they will make are forever.

The religious significance of permanence is linked to the promise that God's love has no limits. If marriage is a sign of God's presence in human life, then it needs to embody the same kind of commitment to love without end that we understand is at the heart of God. The promise that God's love is forever liberates humankind from anxious worry about failing to live up to the conditions of that love. It is a gift freely given without conditions of behavior or time. When two people promise to love each other until death parts them, that promise of permanence creates an environment without conditions. Becoming married is a highly anxious process when one partner threatens to leave if certain conditions are not met, or if both partners expect that concessions or conflicts will even out at the end of each day or week. To be in it for the long haul means that justice has a longer leash. Permanence takes away some of the anxiety about becoming married and thereby enhances the process.

Is It Your Intention?

The issue of intentionality is a theme about marriage that is most prominent in the Roman Catholic understanding of marriage. In most Protestant wedding ceremonies, the intentionality of the couple is sometimes dealt with directly, sometimes indirectly. In the Roman Catholic Rite of Marriage, the question is asked specifically: "Have you come here freely and without reservation to give yourselves to each other in marriage?" The inability to establish intent has been used to keep some people, like the developmentally disabled, from being allowed to marry.

Consent is central to most understandings of marriage. Even in those cultures in which parents still choose a spouse for their child, there must be consent. The action of consenting to marry presumes not only the capacity to make such a choice but also some understanding of the meaning of the action. Marriage is more than a contract. Two people freely choose to enter a covenant for the whole of their lives. This must be done intelligently and responsibly. If it is not, according to Roman Catholic practice, the marriage may be annulled because of a "lack of due discretion" and/or the "incapacity to assume and fulfill the essential obligations of marriage."[8] Because of the practice of annulment in the Roman Catholic tradition, consent and discretion are necessary factors for beginning a marriage.

The ability to commit to the process is an essential element of most every theological understanding of marriage. It is not a process for proxies. Nobody can do it for us. Even if we believe that God determined marriage in the first instance, we do not hold God responsible for our decision to marry. We decide. And we must be able to decide and decide again and again to stay in a relationship that is almost always more complex than we thought at first it would be. The community's support and the promise of God's presence do not take away from our responsibility to intend to marry. Even when there are special pressures to decide for or against marrying or circumstances that complicate the beginning of a marriage, it is our decision. We may fall in love but we do not fall into marriage. That requires a decision.

Most of the decisions we make, however, are influenced by factors outside our awareness. This is certainly true of marriage. We are not fully aware of the ways we expect the one we marry to fulfill unmet needs from our childhood or complete some portion of a self that we think is missing. Our desire to marry the person we choose may be partially hidden from us until we have been married for some time. People who marry need to be prepared to be surprised by the power of buried conflicts, needs, and emotions that surface at unexpected times and places after the wedding. The almost certain discovery in marriage of old patterns of thinking and feeling is one of the reasons post-wedding pastoral care is so essential.

The freedom to choose whom we shall marry is an awesome risk. Because all human freedom is finite, we make choices with lifelong consequences on the basis of limited knowledge. In a way, given how little couples who marry often know about each other, it is remarkable that so many marriages endure. It certainly helps people stay in a marriage if their choice has the blessing of parents and family. The following testimony to the gift of choosing was written by a mother for her son's wedding.

> Choosing is an act of freedom, and a manifestation of desire to become "new again" in new intimacy. On this day of summer newness, we gather to begin a new family, and to celebrate new hope in a troubled world. These two young people are enjoined to become new in many ways—in spirit, in understanding, in behavior, in commitment, and especially in a promise of unending forgiveness to one another and to us. That is the thrust of the Christian message, and also the focus of this ceremony: they are the chosen ones: they have chosen one another, and we are delighted.
>
> (Janet)

The importance of being intentional about marriage supports our conviction that leaving comes before cleaving. Understanding the legacy of our family of origin is one way to increase our freedom to intend marriage. The explorations of our families of origin before the wedding are aimed at making explicit the roles and expectations and emotional claims that might impede as well as enhance our ability to make a commitment to marry. The focus on family of origin will also encourage parents to let go, so that their son or daughter is free to intend to begin a family of his or her own. Some recovery of a ritual of betrothal or family blessing would enhance this process of letting go.

Take This Ring as Sign of my Love and Fidelity

When we think about fidelity in relation to marriage, the focus is often on sexual intimacy. It is that, of course, but it is much more. Faithfulness has many meanings. It is about the promises we keep and choices we make for the sake of forging a marital bond. In that sense, fidelity is about thinking of "we" as well as "I." Faithfulness is about promising again and then promising again to promise again. Because we have committed to be with another person in an enduring relationship, letting go of our own preferences, our own will, our own desires all become instances of faithfulness. "I give you this ring as a sign of my vow, and with all that I am, and all that I have, I honor you."[9] Being faithful to another human being transcends or changes all other obligations, including obligations to the family of our origin.

Faithfulness is more than a pledge to a person; it is a commitment to marriage itself. Here is how Dietrich Bonhoeffer said it in his wedding sermon from a prison cell: "As high as God is above us, so high are the sanctity, the rights, and the promise of marriage above the sanctity, the rights, and the promise of love. It is not your love that sustains the marriage, but from now on, the marriage that sustains your love."[10] Our commitment is not just to our spouse but to the institution of marriage as well. Marriage is more than something two people do. It is a pledge of faithfulness on the part of the assembly to sustain these two people in their work to become married.

Being faithful is something we do rather than something we possess. And it is what we do when we commit and recommit ourselves to the process of becoming married. We are committed to staying in the process as a consequence of our vows to a person. This is the most difficult faithfulness of all because the results are not always certain. Therefore, we need to be open to change in order to be faithful to a process that will most

certainly eventuate in something new that neither could anticipate when we began it.[11]

That They May Surely Keep Their Marriage Covenant

Covenant is one of the most common theological images
of marriage. The declaration of marriage in one wedding ceremony includes these lines: "You have declared your consent
and vows before God and this congregation. May God confirm
your covenant and fill you both with grace."[12] The marriage relationship is, above all else, covenantal in nature. It is grounded
in the promises that we make to each other and the fidelity that
is both the form and the substance of those promises. The biblical theologian Walter Brueggemann has suggested that marriage is an exercise of faithfulness in which every dimension of
life is enhanced by the vows we keep. According to Brueggemann, marriage is not based on romantic or erotic feelings, but
on "the readiness to take the covenant partner in abiding seriousness."[13] Love is being loyal to the promises we make.

Tak[ing] the covenant partner in abiding seriousness is an
apt summary of what we have been saying throughout this volume on the nature of the marital bond. While people are drawn
to each other through erotic or romantic attraction, it is covenantal love that sustains a couple in the process of becoming married when the going gets rough. When the idealized picture of a
spouse begins to fade, it is loyalty to promises made that encourages us to deepen our understanding and acceptance of the other.
When conflicting needs and expectations emerge, it is fidelity to
a covenant partner that keeps us looking for ways to honor each
other without sacrificing either.

Marriage is understood as a religious covenant because
we believe God is present to sustain this union with grace and
love. In that sense, it is more than a bond between a woman and
a man. God is a partner in the marital bond. This understanding
of marriage as covenant is an extension of the biblical story that
looks at all reality in covenantal terms. Covenant embodies
both the relationship between God and humankind and the goal

for all human relationships. Although human folk have not found it easy to keep covenant, there is a need inherent in creation that draws us to one another and to God.

Covenantal relationships, as Brueggemann reminds us, are based on vows freely taken. They are established in mutuality and shaped by the particular context rather than prescribed by absolute forms. They are long on promises and possibilities and short on guarantees. A covenant is not a contract. A covenant is sustained by fidelity rather than legal stipulations or contractual obligations. And fidelity provides covenant with an anchor that no prescription can match for durability.

This theme of marriage as covenant is particularly important for our time. There is no doubt that becoming married is more complex for many people today who have professional careers and financial assets to fit together in a common life. The specter of divorce has motivated many couples to establish a contract before marrying about how assets will be dispersed if the marriage should not endure. But contracts do not make covenants. Thinking about marriage as covenant enhances bonding because it is a reminder of our vow to hold our partner in abiding seriousness.

Between Past Legacies and Future Visions

We have emphasized throughout this volume the importance of understanding our origins as a way to get ready for marriage. Most of all that means an awareness of the legacy that we bring to a marriage from our families of origin. The aim of that awareness is not the rejection of our origins. Nor does leaving home mean ignoring our past. We simply need to be aware of the powerful claim that those origins continue to exercise on our life outside that family in order to increase our freedom to intend to marry. We understand the stories of our origins in order that they might become a resource for becoming married.

In addition to this legacy from our families, each of us has some internalized expectation of marriage that will affect the process of becoming married that we intend. Our picture of marriage may be a replica of our parents' marriage. More often, however, it is a composite of people we have known and the images from the common culture that promote romanticism and reinforce individualism. We all have some internalized personal understanding of what marriage means. However vague or unformed these images of marriage might be, they are part of the past we bring to marriage. Making overt what have been covert pictures is an important part of getting ready for the wedding.

What we have learned from our religious traditions about the meaning of marriage may not be explicit until we begin preparing for the wedding. It is nonetheless part of our common past. Even when marriage is being done differently or at least not thought about in religious categories, permanence and fidelity and covenant are still issues that have to be confronted. Planning for the wedding is in part instruction. It is important to help couples identify their hidden, operational theologies or beliefs at the same time that we articulate the current theologies of marriage. Our aim is to help them become aware of the legacies from their past that will influence the process of becoming married.

The wedding ceremony not only recapitulates the past; it anticipates the future. We need to know where we have come from. We also need to know where we are going. The Danish philosopher Søren Kierkegaard once observed that we understand our lives looking backward but we live our lives looking forward. Part of planning the wedding is to help couples "look forward" to the kind of family they would like to become (see chapter 2). To that end, we work with them to select images or themes from their religious traditions that might give direction to their bonding process. Because these themes need not be specifically about marriage, they represent a theology *for* marriage as distinct from a theology *of* marriage.

Becoming married from a Christian perspective is more than bonding or making a marriage. It is forming a *marital habitus*. We use the ancient word "habitus" to emphasize that the final goal of becoming married is a way of being together. Habitus is the "disposition of the soul" that is both practical and theological, because it directs and guides how we live. Every marriage has both good and bad habits. It is the way we are with each other in marriage that is so habitual that we are not always conscious of how we respond. We are suggesting a theological framework for encouraging good habits in marriage. A marital habitus is both how a couple relate to one another *and* how they live in the world as a couple. Being married is not like a coat we can put on or take off. It is not a sometime thing. A marital habitus is the way a couple live together that flows from the conviction that marriage is an unfolding covenant. It is like breathing.

Marks of a Marital Habitus

There are many themes from our faith traditions that couples might choose as a goal for their life together. (See Appendix B for a suggested list of biblical passages that couples might use to develop a vision for their life together.) We have selected five themes from the Christian tradition that embody for us a covenantal understanding of relationships. They expand what it means "to take the covenant partner in abiding seriousness." They are qualities of a marital habitus: sacrifice, justice, reconciliation, hospitality, and joy. Each of these themes has implications for the couple's life together *and* their life as a couple in the world. They point in the direction of a theology *for* marriage.

While some of our themes for a marital habitus are referred to only indirectly, the letter to the Philippians suggests a spirituality for faithful living and friendship that is a vision for being married. Philippians is not a text explicitly about marriage but an intimate epistle on the Christian life. Even so, "the letter is replete with language and concerns drawn from the ancient topic of friendship" that reflect Paul's deeply personal relationship with the church at Philippi.[14] Both the tone and the content fit a habitus for marriage. It is a letter about covenantal living. Although we have not used the metaphor of friendship to describe the marital bond, the themes of mutuality, partnership, and reciprocity are common to both. The letter begins in a spirit of gratitude ("I thank my God every time I remember you . . . ," Phil. 1:3) that is a poignant expression of what it could mean for a wife or husband to *take the covenant partner in abiding seriousness.*

Sacrifice

Covenantal relationships call for sacrifice because they recognize the value in another human being and they promise fidelity to the other. Sacrifice is the willingness to forgo the benefits of particular choices for the sake of another's well-being because we hold that person in abiding seriousness. The deeper meaning of sacrifice is not about giving up but about giving over our freedom to a larger reality. It is an aspect of benevolence. In the case of marriage, that common bond is the relationship. If mutuality and equal regard characterize the way in which two distinct persons make choices in a marriage, sacrifice is inevitable. It is not just a corrective to an imbalance but a necessary dimension of any relationship that seeks for equal regard.

The admonition from Paul about sacrifice is direct and unambiguous. "Do nothing from selfish ambition or conceit, but in humility regard others as better than yourselves. Let each of you look not to your own interests, but to the interests of others" (2:3–4). Having the mind of Christ leads to a willingness to set aside our needs for the needs of others. This is true for marriage as well as any human community. There has been an understandable sensitivity recently about suggesting sacrifice in marriage, because we have assumed for a long time that women were the primary accommodators in family living. However, when wives and husbands hold each other in abiding faithfulness, they will each be committed to the interests of each other.

Sacrifice has been necessary throughout human history, but it is particularly crucial for our time because the choices that couples have are multiplying. No one can have it all if the marriage is to be just. From the beginning of a relationship, couples today will need to make decisions that include sacrifice. When a career opportunity in another geographic location is offered to one partner and the dislocation necessary to accept the offer seriously disrupts the life or career of the other partner, sacrifice is required. These decisions may not balance out immediately. Moreover, sacrifices that deepen the marital habitus are not recorded on a score card. They are determined by the promise each partner makes to hold the other in abiding seriousness *and* honor the larger vision of being together in marriage. Couples who do volunteer work together on behalf of a social need reinforce the practice of sacrifice that is part of their life together.

We will explore more fully the implications of sacrifice for family living in *Raising Children,* the next volume in this series. Preoccupation with marital happiness may be at a child's expense. Barbara Defoe Whitehead has said it very clearly: "All too often the adult quest for freedom, independence, and choice in family relationships conflicts with a child's developmental needs for stability, constancy, harmony, and permanence in family life."[15] The sacrificial choices that couples learn to make as they become married will create an environment in which it will be possible for them to set aside their interests for the well-being of the children.

Justice

Sacrifice deepens the marital habitus as long as it is just. When one partner does all the accommodating or when the sacrifices are unevenly distributed over time, the covenant of mutuality is distorted and the marriage is not just. The marriage may be stable. It may even be a happy relationship. But it is not just. The insistence that opportunities for growth and self-determination are available to women as well as men is an illustration of justice in marriage. A balanced distribution of power and the maintenance of equal regard are both necessary if we are to establish covenantal relationships that are just. Marriages that endure are able to keep alive the paradox of self-determination and sacrifice.

The issue of justice usually surfaces early in the process of becoming married. Dating patterns are often an early signal about the exercise of power. Sometimes it is evident even before the wedding that one family of origin will seek to influence the developing bond more than the other. Planning who and how many are invited to the wedding is an early exercise for the couple in making just decisions. All of that occurs before a couple must decide whose job to live closer to, whose family of origin to spend more time with, whose coffeemaker to use, whose sleeping temperature to accommodate, whose subscriptions to continue, and countless other issues. When the choices were fewer and the patterns of accommodation clearer, the issue of justice in marriage seemed simpler.

Righteousness is God's saving work, of that Paul was sure. It comes to women and men of faith as a gift because of the death and resurrection of Jesus Christ. And yet we are to strain forward to what lies ahead "toward the goal for the prize of the heavenly call of God in Christ Jesus" (3:14). In that spirit, the recipients of the letter to the Philippians are urged to do "whatever is just" (4:8) as well as pure and honorable and pleasing and true and commendable. What makes justice different for those who follow Christ is that it is something that is given rather than something that is earned. It is impossible to separate justice from gratitude.

If the paradox of family living is to honor in a balanced way *both* the needs of the individual *and* the needs of the community, then self-sacrificial love as the final norm of the Christian life does not alone provide an adequate framework for a habitus for marriage. The Belgian Roman Catholic moral theologian Louis Janssens has proposed an intriguing alternative. Mutuality in the sense of equal regard, Janssens suggests, is the normative meaning of Christian love.[16] Equal regard in marriage means that we are to take the needs of our neighbor-spouse with as much seriousness as our own. The self-determination of a husband or a wife is equal—but no more than equal—to the self-determination of his wife or her husband.

This concern for mutuality is particularly necessary for husbands and wives who must balance in a just manner the obligations of career and children as well as the demands of hobbies and community. Justice is not a solution but a way of being. It is a habitus that requires a second look. There is an ancient meaning of respect that links justice with recognition. A quick glance will not do. Looking long enough to see the other in his or her uniqueness takes the other in abiding seriousness. Taking a second look will also enable the couple to see and respond to the world outside themselves. Because our own needs and the needs of spouse, children, or aging parents as well as the needs of the world usually exceed our finite energies and time, we will regularly need to make decisions that require sacrifice.

Reconciliation

If we understand the personal maturity that is required to be promise keepers, if we are clear about the complexity of sacrifice and the ambiguity of justice, we will not be surprised that covenantal relationships are full of broken promises. We are fragile, imperfect people struggling to fulfill our humanness. And we fail. Covenantal relationships are the occasion and the expression of that humanness. There is a sense in which we are most known to be sinners in our families. Because human sin is an inescapable reality, the promise and possibility of reconciliation must be part of a marital habitus.

Promises are kept and promises are broken in any marriage. Some are broken unintentionally, some intentionally. The possibility of reconciliation in marriage is determined not so much by the severity of the break as by the depth of the will to reconcile and be reconciled. The practice of reconciliation in a marriage is an extension of the *readiness to take the covenantal partner in abiding seriousness*. Taking another person seriously means acknowledging the violation and experiencing the pain of a promise broken. In response to broken promises, reconciliation is not a hasty peace. It means inviting and receiving the forgiveness that is inherent in the promise to be true to one another in good times and bad. In the end, however, reconciliation is more than righting wrongs. It brings us to a deeper place of trust and commitment.

There was dissension among the Christians in Philippi that troubled Paul deeply. Euodia and Syntyche are encouraged to come to "be of the same mind in the Lord" (Phil. 4:2). Over and over again the Christians at Philippi are encouraged to be united and strive "side by side with one mind for the faith of the gospel" (1:27). Such unity is not an end in itself. It is necessary in order not to be overcome by the opponents of the gospel. In a similar way, couples need to strive to be "side by side" in their relationship in order to withstand pressures from the world that would undermine their fragile bond. We do not suggest antagonism on the part of a couple toward whatever is outside the marriage but a healthy respect for the social and cultural forces that mandates reconciliation as a way of being married. Creating a peaceable marriage is a way of demonstrating to the world the transforming love of God in human life.

Reconciliation is an essential characteristic of the habitus of marriage today, not only because the gladness of marriage is frequently overcast with the burden of sin but because honoring the diversity of our lives inevitably leads to greater conflict. Because more people marry across cultures as well as race and religion, the traditions we bring to forming a marital bond are increasingly different. If we learn to recognize the uniqueness of the other in the relationship, and if we honor the differences between women and men, there will be tension in a marital bond. Those differences may indeed add to the richness of marriage. They may also lead to conflict. In order that we might benefit from the gifts that diversity brings to a relationship, we need to practice reconciling as a dimension of our being together.

Hospitality

A relationship in which sacrifice, justice, and reconciliation prevail is likely to be a hospitable environment. It will be a community that is safe for oneself and the other, where trust and mutual respect invite the fullest humanness possible. The signs of a hospitable environment are deceptively simple. It is a context in which affirmation is unconditional and expectations are explicit. It is a holding environment in which there is freedom to have "a room of one's own" and freedom to be together. It is a context in which even the "stranger within" each marital partner may be received.

The Christians in Philippi had been generous in their support of Paul. In a way that deviated from his normal practice, Paul trusted that this community's support would not be used to dominate or coerce. His letter is an expression of his gratitude for their hospitality. What makes Paul's response significant for our consideration of hospitality as a characteristic of family living is that he begins in humility. "I know what it is to have little, and I know what it is to have plenty. In any and all circumstances I have learned the secret of being well-fed and of going hungry, of having plenty and of being in need" (Phil. 4:12). Our capacity for hospitality is a consequence of being recipients of God's generosity. Husbands and wives are able to be hospitable and generous with each other when they believe they have enough already.

The invitation to hospitality does not stop at the boundaries of the marital relationship. It extends to the nearby neighbor and to the larger community of which the marriage is a part. Marriage is a public reality. When a couple insulate themselves from the larger community, when they do not extend hospitality outward, they threaten the foundation of their bond. The invisible boundaries that a couple create around their relationship in order to nurture and strengthen it need to be permeable enough to encourage appropriate connections to the larger world. Withdrawal for restoration and recreation is a necessary part of the rhythm of marriage. Being faithful to that rhythm means returning to the openness that makes others welcome.

Joy

The opening invocation of the marriage rite in the Episcopal Church includes this phrase: "The union of husband and wife in heart, body, and mind is intended by God for their mutual joy."[17] We have said in many ways that marriage is hard work, that it requires an intentionality that is sometimes difficult to sustain in a complex society. It is also clear, however, that being married is an experience of mutual joy that comes from knowing that one can love and be loved. This joy goes deeper than happiness. It is the pleasure of giving and receiving sexual pleasure. It is the endless wonder and surprise that these two people who share this bed and this table find in their company with each other. It is a mirror of God's delight in human love that is mutual.

The Christian tradition has been reluctant to acknowledge the gift of sensuous feelings and unabashed delight of erotic love. Nor have we been inclined to develop a theology that honors pleasure as an appropriate aim in human life. We are keenly aware of the way desire can be abused to seek only its own fulfillment. But it need not always be so. The experience of desire and pleasure is a way of connecting with another human being. When one meets the other in pleasure, the meeting serves nothing else. It is simply for the sake of being with another in pleasure. The sexual bond that is necessary to sustain marriage is not likely to endure without pleasure. And the freedom to celebrate erotic love depends on an enduring commitment.

The spirit of joy that pervades Paul's letter to the saints at Philippi is amazing when one remembers that it was written from prison and to a struggling community. Paul had found a peace from God "which surpasses all understanding" (4:7). For Paul, having that peace did not depend on freedom or success or even safety. For married couples today, that peace does not depend on having a room of one's own or obedient children or even sexual pleasure. What Paul knew and we need to know is that the peace and joy that endure are a by-product of faithful living. The joy we experience is not our own. It is from God. This joy is a gift given to those who have learned to hold and be held in abiding seriousness. When we keep doing that, we will also discover the joy in being married. It is the springtime of marriage against all winters.

SYMBOLS FOR GENOGRAMS

THE FOLLOWING format is adapted from standards recommended by the Task Force of the North American Primary Care Research Group and outlined in *Genograms in Family Assessment*, by Monica McGoldrick and Randy Gerson (New York: W. W. Norton & Co., 1985), pages 154–155.

A. Symbols to Describe Basic Family Membership

Male: ☐   Female: ○   Birth date ➝ 43–75 ◄— Death date
⊠ X = Death

Marriage (give date) (Husband on left, wife on right): ☐—m. 60—○

Living together relationship or liaison: ☐—72—○

Marital separation (give date): ☐—s. 70—○

Divorce (give date): ☐—d. 72—○

Children: List in birth order, beginning with oldest on left: 60 | 62 | 65

Adopted or foster children:

Fraternal twins:

Identical twins:

Pregnancy:

3 mos.

Spontaneous abortion:

Induced abortion:

Stillbirth:

B. Diagraming Family Interaction Patterns

Very close relationship:

Conflictual relationship:

Distant relationship:

Estrangement or cut off (give dates if possible):

Cut off 62–78

Fused and conflictual:

C. Family Information of Special Importance

Since the genogram is intended to be an orienting map for the family, it is useful to include significant events or problems or patterns over generations.

1. Religious history
2. Major or chronic illnesses
3. Ethnic background
4. Education
5. Occupation or work outside the home
6. Alcoholism or other substance abuse
7. Unresolved conflicts across generations
8. Trouble with the law
9. Coincidences of loss and history of grief
10. The significance of names and nicknames

11. Major triangles in the family system
12. Physical or sexual abuse
13. Role of women
14. Who are the strong ones in the tradition
15. Relationships to major events in world history
16. Secrets and secret keepers
17. Leaving-home patterns
18. Major disappointments or unfulfilled dreams
19. Affairs
20. Attitudes about money
21. Impact of divorce
22. Who received special blessings

D.   Governing Belief or Myth System for the Family

It is useful to listen for particular images or metaphors that reflect what a family values. Sometimes those beliefs can be discovered by inviting people to recall family sayings or maxims. Sometimes they are evident in the way a person describes his or her family's story. It is appropriate simply to note a word or a phrase on the genogram that reflects the family's assumptive world.

SCRIPTURE TEXTS FOR WEDDINGS

A WIDE RANGE of scripture texts is available from which the couple may make selections to be read at their ceremony. Those texts usually have some reference to love or marriage or relations between women and men, and therefore support a particular understanding of marriage. If, however, the readings are to reflect the kind of family the couple would like to become, then the text might address a larger theme of the Christian life, such as hospitality or justice or peacemaking. The following list of texts suggests both kinds of reading—those directly referring to marriage and those that point to Christian living in marriage. We have included a number of texts that are suggested in *Scripture at Weddings: Choosing and Proclaiming the Word of God*, by Graziano Marcheschi with Nancy Seitz Marcheschi (Chicago: Liturgy Training Publications, 1992).

Genesis 1:26–28, 31; 2:18–24	The creation of man and woman
Song of Solomon	(Portions may be read by the bride and the groom to each other as part of the service)
Isaiah 43:16–21	God is doing a new thing—can we see it?

Jeremiah 31:31–34	"I will be their God and they . . . my people"
Ecclesiasticus 25:1, 2ff.	Husband and wife who are inseparable
Tobit 8:5–7	Growing old together
Matthew 5:1–12	"Blessed are the peacemakers"
5:13–16	"You are the light of the world"
22:35–40	"You shall love your neighbor as yourself"
Mark 8:1–9	God will provide enough for the journey
John 2:1–11	"There was a wedding in Cana of Galilee"
John 15:9–16	"Love one another as I have loved you"
Romans 12:1–2, 9–18	Be generous in offering hospitality
1 Corinthians 13	No limit to love's endurance
Colossians 3:12–17	Qualities of living for God's people
1 John 3:18–24	Love in truth and action
4:7–16	"Love one another, because love is from God"

NOTES

▽

Introduction

1. A clear articulation of the tension between marriages that intend to be mutual and the expectations of a market society can be found in Ulrich Beck, *The Risk Society: Towards a New Modernity*, trans. Mark Ritter (Newbury Park, Calif.: Sage Publications, 1992), 103–26.

2. Robert F. Stahmann and William J. Hiebert, *Premarital Counseling: The Professional's Handbook*, 2d ed. (Lexington, Mass.: D. C. Heath & Co., 1987), 3–16.

3. The most comprehensive and widely used of these instruments is *PrepareEnrich,* developed by David H. Olson, David G. Fournier, and Joan M. Druckman (Prepare-Enrich, Inc., P. O. Box 190, Minneapolis, MN 55440). The aim of this inventory is to help couples become more aware of their relationship strengths and begin resolving some of their relationship issues. Another inventory used in premarital preparation is the Taylor-Johnson Temperament Analysis Profile. It measures nine bipolar personality characteristics and provides a way to measure the accuracy of each one's perception of the other. For a comprehensive listing of the inventories in premarital counseling, see Stahmann and Hiebert, *Premarital Counseling*, 207–41. While each of these inventories has value in identifying the issues in a relationship, it is our judgment that the focus on the couple is more productive after the wedding, when the process of becoming married is the publicly declared intent of the couple.

Chapter 1. Leaving Comes Before Cleaving

1. Herbert Anderson and Kenneth R. Mitchell, *Leaving Home*, Family Living in Pastoral Perspective (Louisville, Ky.: Westminster/John Knox Press, 1993), 26.

2. The phenomenon of "nonfamily residential autonomy" has become a new symbol of adulthood affecting both leaving home and becoming mar-

ried. In *Leaving Home Before Marriage* (Madison: University of Wisconsin Press, 1993), Frances K. Goldscheider and Calvin Goldscheider show that a substantial majority of young people (70%) expect to live independently of parents before marriage even though they may be unrealistic about the costs. Even so, the Goldscheiders conclude, "it is not yet clearly institutionalized as a way-station in young adulthood" (186).

3. There are a variety of reasons that people marry today, and romantic love is still one of them. Falling in love does not seem to correlate with either age or duration of marriage. According to Andrew Greeley's study *Love and Marriage*, men are more romantic than women. "Romantic love may be necessary for marriage to occur, but it surely is not necessary to sustain the marriage relationship, which is based on more durable, less ephemeral qualities" (Andrew Greeley, *Faithful Attraction: Discovering Intimacy, Love, and Fidelity in American Marriage* [New York: Tom Doherty Associates, 1991], 122). See also Marsha Lasswell and Norman M. Lobsenz, *Styles of Loving* (New York: Ballantine Books, 1980).

4. Anderson and Mitchell, *Leaving Home,* 73–74.

5. John Hersey, "The Announcement," in *Atlantic Monthly,* December 1989, 96.

6. Martin Luther, *Luther's Works: The Christian in Society II* (Philadelphia: Muhlenberg Press, 1962), 381–93.

7. Steven Ozment, *When Fathers Ruled: Family Life in Reformation Europe* (Cambridge, Mass.: Harvard University Press, 1983), 41.

8. Robert Bellah, *Habits of the Heart: Individualism and Commitment in American Life* (Berkeley, Calif.: University of California Press, 1985), 107.

9. Kenneth J. Gergen, "The Saturated Family," in *The Family Therapy Networker* 15, no. 5 (September-October 1991): 30.

10. Ulrich Beck, *The Risk Society: Towards a New Modernity,* trans. Mark Ritter (Newbury Park, Calif.: Sage Publications, 1992), 135.

11. Gerhard von Rad, *Genesis: A Commentary* (Philadelphia: Westminster Press, 1961), 83.

12. For a very accessible resource on early Christian thought on marriage, see *Marriage in the Early Church,* trans. and ed. David G. Hunter (Minneapolis: Fortress Press, 1992).

13. Dianne Bergant, C.S.A., "Partners in the Mystery of Creation," in *Where Can We Find Her?,* ed. Marie-Eloise Rosenblatt, R.S.M. (Mahwah, N.J.: Paulist Press, 1991), 18.

Chapter 2. A Wedding of Stories

1. This image of marriage as a wedding of stories was developed by Herbert Anderson and Edward Foley, O.F.M. Cap., in "A Wedding of Stories," *New Theology Review* 3, no. 2 (May 1990). For further reading on the impact of families of origin on being married, see James L. Framo, *Family-of-Origin Therapy: An Intergenerational Approach* (New York: Brunner/Mazel, 1992), and Harriet Goldner Lerner, *The Dance of Intimacy* (New York: Harper & Row, 1989).

2. Story is a particularly useful vehicle for identifying and understanding the legacy that each has received from his or her family of origin. See Robert Coles, *The Call of Stories* (Boston: Houghton Mifflin Co., 1989) and Charles Gerkin, *Widening the Horizons: Pastoral Responses to a Fragmented Society* (Philadelphia: Westminster Press, 1986), esp. ch. 2, "Stories and *The Story*: Narrative Theology and the Task of Pastoral Care."

3. Evan Imber-Black, ed., *Secrets in Families and Family Therapy* (New York: W.W. Norton & Co., 1993), especially "Shame: Reservoir for Family Secrets," 29–43.

4. John Dominic Crossan, *The Dark Interval: Towards a Theology of Story* (Sonoma, Calif.: Polebridge Press, 1988).

5. Norman Paul's theory of the negative impact of buried grief on a family over generations continues to be a useful insight. See Norman Paul and Betty Paul, *The Marital Puzzle* (New York: W.W. Norton & Co., 1975).

6. Kenneth R. Mitchell and Herbert Anderson, "You Must Leave Before You Can Cleave," *Pastoral Psychology* 30, no. 2, (Winter 1981): 71–88. Monica McGoldrick has said it well: "Weddings are meant to be transition rituals that facilitate family process. As such they are extremely important for marking the change in status of family members and the shifting in family organization." (*The Changing Family Life Cycle,* 2d edition, ed. Betty Carter and Monica McGoldrick [New York: Gardner Press, 1988], 222.)

7. Monica McGoldrick and Randy Gerson, *Genograms in Family Assessment* (New York: W.W. Norton & Co., 1985). See also Emily Marlin, *Genograms* (Chicago: Contemporary Books, 1989).

8. We are indebted to the Rev. David Schaeffer, D. Min., for this case. As with all the cases, the names and details of the story have been altered to maintain confidentiality.

9. Froma Walsh, "The Timing of Symptoms and Critical Events in the Family Life Cycle," in *Clinical Implications of the Family Life Cycle*, ed. James C. Hanson (Rockville, Md.: Aspen Systems Corporation, 1983). For a more extensive treatment of death in the family see Froma Walsh and Monica McGoldrick, eds., *Living Beyond Loss* (New York: W. W. Norton & Co., 1991).

Chapter 3. Planning A Meaningful Wedding

1. A very useful guide to planning the wedding ritual is Sidney F. Batts, *The Protestant Wedding Sourcebook: A Complete Guide for Developing Your Own Service* (Louisville, Ky.: Westminster/John Knox Press, 1993). For a consideration of the family dynamics in planning a wedding, see Edwin Friedman, *Generation to Generation: Family Process in Church and Synagogue* (New York: Guilford Press, 1985).

2. Several books have appeared recently that reflect a renewed awareness of the need for ritual in human life. See Evan Imber-Black, Janine Roberts, and Richard Whiting, eds., *Rituals in Families and Family Ther-*

apy (New York: W.W. Norton & Co., 1988); Evan Imber-Black and Janine Roberts, eds., *Rituals for Our Times* (New York: HarperCollins, 1992); and Tom F. Driver, *The Magic of Ritual: Our Need for Liberating Rites That Transform Our Lives & Our Communities* (San Francisco: HarperCollins, 1991).

3. Ron Grimes, unpublished manuscript.

4. Kenneth W. Stevenson, *To Join Together: The Rite of Marriage* (New York: Pueblo Publishing Co., 1987).

5. Gilbert Ostdick, "Human Situations in Need of Ritualization," *New Theology Review* 3, no. 2 (May 1990): 36–50.

6. Arnold van Gennep, *The Rites of Passage* (Chicago: University of Chicago Press, 1960). See Edwin H. Friedman, "Systems and Ceremonies: A Family View of Rites of Passage," in *The Changing Family Life Cycle,* ed. Betty Carter and Monica McGoldrick (New York: Gardner Press, 1988), 119–47.

7. Nico ter Linden, personal correspondence.

8. Rainer Maria Rilke, *Rilke on Love and Other Difficulties*, ed. John Mood (New York: W. W. Norton & Co., 1975), 28.

9. Ibid. This theme of honoring separateness is developed in a splendid philosophical essay by Ilham Dilman titled *Love and Human Separateness* (Oxford: Basil Blackwell Publisher, 1987). It is separateness, he says, that "underlies the possibility of all forms of intimacy in which we make contact with another human being—in sexual love and friendship" (107).

10. Dietrich Bonhoeffer, *Letters and Papers from Prison*, ed. Eberhard Bethge (New York: Macmillan Publishing Co., 1972), 43.

11. Ron Grimes, unpublished manuscript.

Chapter 4. When the Ordinary Is Complicated

1. See Herbert Anderson, *The Family and Pastoral Care* (Philadelphia: Fortress Press, 1984) for a fuller discussion of the gift of diversity and family living.

2. Charles Gerkin, "On the Art of Caring," *The Journal of Pastoral Care* 45, no. 4 (Winter 1991). The role and necessity of pastoral advocacy in working with families is a distinctive theme throughout this series. Larry Kent Graham has suggested that the "pastoral caregiver, as advocate, uses his or her power position to share the risks of changing the social order, and lends to the directions for necessary change" (*Care of Persons, Care of Worlds* [Nashville: Abingdon Press, 1992], 47). In this volume we are also describing as advocacy those pastoral interventions in which the caregiver acts on behalf of an individual for the sake of change within the family system.

3. Nicholas S. Aradi, "Toward a Conceptualization and Treatment of Interfaith Marriage," in *Couples Therapy in a Family Context: Perspective and Retrospective*, ed. Florence W. Kaslow (Rockville, Md.: Aspen Publishers, 1988).

4. Matthijs Kalmijn, "Shifting Boundaries: Trends in Religious and Educational Homogamy," *American Sociological Review* 56 (December 1991): 798. See also Michael Lawler, *Ecumenical Marriage & Remarriage: Gifts and Challenges to the Churches* (Mystic, Conn.: Twenty-third Publications, 1990). Lawler regards marriages between persons of different faith traditions as a positive opportunity for Christian unity.

5. Mark Methabane and Gail Methabane, *Love in Black and White: The Triumph of Love over Prejudice and Taboo* (New York: HarperCollins, 1992).

6. Kenneth R. Mitchell and Herbert Anderson, *All Our Losses, All Our Griefs* (Philadelphia: Westminster Press, 1983), 94–95.

7. Betty Carter and Monica McGoldrick, *The Changing Family Life Cycle* (New York: Gardner Press, 1988), 402.

8. Froma Walsh and Monica McGoldrick, eds., *Living Beyond Loss* (New York: W. W. Norton & Co., 1991), 219–21.

9. Eleanor D. Macklin, "Nonmarital Heterosexual Cohabitation: An Overview," in *Contemporary Families and Alternative Lifestyles*, ed. Eleanor D. Macklin and Roger H. Rubin, (Beverly Hills, Calif.: Sage Publications, 1983).

10. The issue of cohabitation is of concern to religious communities primarily in relation to sexual intercourse. Even though the sexuality of all persons is affirmed, most church traditions insist that "sexual relations are only clearly affirmed in the marriage bond." Some traditions take a pastoral approach to the practice of living together outside of marriage, whereas others regard it as an "unholy substitute." For further information about the position of particular churches on this matter, see J. Gordon Melton, *Sex and Family Life: Official Statements from Religious Bodies and Ecumenical Organizations* (Detroit: Gale Research, 1991).

Chapter 5. Getting Married Changes Things

1. Judith Viorst, *Necessary Losses* (New York: Simon & Schuster, 1986), 180.

2. Harville Hendrix, *Getting the Love You Want* (New York: Henry Holt, 1988). We enter marriage, Hendrix suggests, with the expectation that our partner will fulfill unmet needs and heal wounds that linger from our families of origin. What we call romantic love has much to do with this longing for wholeness and restoration.

3. Robert Bellah, *Habits of the Heart: Individualism and Commitment in American Life* (Berkeley: University of California Press, 1985), 107. Bellah says it this way: "For the classic utilitarian individualist, the only valid contract is one based on negotiation between individuals acting in their own self-interest. . . . No binding obligations and no wider social understanding justify a relationship. It exists only as the expression of the choices of the free selves who make it up. And should it no longer meet their needs, it must end."

4. Kenneth R. Mitchell, "Tacit Contracts," *Pastoral Psychology*, March 1972, 7–18. See Clifford J. Sager, M.D., *Marriage Contracts and Couple Therapy: Hidden Forces in Intimate Relationships* (New York: Brunner/ Mazel, 1976). Sager identifies three levels of contracts that are likely to occur in marriage: conscious, verbalized; conscious, but not yet verbalized; beyond awareness.

5. Deborah Tannen, *You Just Don't Understand: Women and Men in Conversation* (New York: Ballantine Books, 1990). Men and women not only experience the world differently, they speak about what they experience differently. The aim of Tannen's book corresponds with our emphasis on honoring uniqueness: "If we can sort out differences based on conversational style, we will be in a better position to confront real conflicts of interest—and to find a shared language in which to negotiate them" (p. 18).

6. Communication patterns in marriage, family therapist Augustus Y. Napier has observed, inevitably reveal the underlying emotional structure of a relationship. Napier's book *The Fragile Bond: In Search of an Equal, Intimate, and Enduring Marriage* (New York: Harper & Row, 1988) is an eloquent testimony to the hard, vulnerable work of making a marriage. For a more specific discussion of the influence of family of origin on patterns of marital communication, see *The First Two Years of Marriage* (Ramsey, N.J.: Paulist Press, 1983).

7. Jessica Benjamin, *The Bonds of Love: Psychoanalysis, Feminism, and the Problem of Domination* (New York: Pantheon Books, 1988), 12.

8. Ibid.

9. Ibid., 221.

Chapter 6. A Covenant of Abiding Seriousness

1. Michael Lawler, *Secular Marriage, Christian Sacrament* (Mystic, Conn.: Twenty-Third Publications, 1985), 77.

2. Vigen Guroian, *Incarnate Love: Essays in Orthodox Ethics,* (South Bend, Ind.: University of Notre Dame Press, 1987), 81.

3. William Johnson Everett, *Blessed Be the Bond: Christian Perspectives on Marriage and Family* (Philadelphia: Fortress Press, 1985), 92.

4. Nico ter Linden, personal correspondence.

5. Edward Schillebeeckx, *Marriage: Human Reality and Saving Mystery* (New York: Sheed & Ward, 1965).

6. Evelyn Eaton Whitehead and James D. Whitehead, *Marrying Well: Stages on the Journey of Christian Marriage* (New York: Image Books, 1983), 124.

7. Ibid., 442.

8. David F. O'Conner, S.T., "Discretion and Capacity for Marriage: Some Canonical and Pastoral Reflections," in *New Theology Review* 2, no. 4 (1989): 61–74.

9. *The Book of Services* (Nashville: United Methodist Publishing House, 1985).

10. Dietrich Bonhoeffer, *Letters and Papers from Prison*, ed. Eberhard Bethge (New York: Macmillan Publishing Co., 1972), 43.

11. One of our favorite texts for a wedding homily is Isaiah 43:18–19: "Do not remember the former things, or consider the things of old. I am about to do a new thing; now it springs forth, do you not perceive it?" This affirmation that God is making something new in marriage is in striking contrast to a slightly jaundiced but unfortunately accurate saying of family therapist Carl Whitaker: "There is no such thing as marriage; families simply elect scapegoats to reproduce themselves." Speaking a word in the homily about the "new thing God is doing" in this marriage is another way to be an advocate for the couple.

12. *The Book of Services* (Nashville: United Methodist Publishing House, 1985).

13. Walter Brueggemann, "The Covenanted Family: A Zone for Humanness," *Journal of Current Social Issues* 14, no. 1 (Winter 1977): 24.

14. John T. Fitzgerald, "Philippians," *The Anchor Bible Dictionary*, ed. David Noel Friedman, vol. 5 (New York: Doubleday, 1992), 320. See L. Michael White, "Morality Between Two Worlds: A Paradigm of Friendship in Philippians," in *Greeks, Romans, and Christians,* ed. David L. Balch, Everitt Fergerson, and Wayne A. Meeks (Minneapolis: Fortress Press, 1990), 201–15.

15. Barbara Defoe Whitehead, "Dan Quayle Was Right," *Atlantic Monthly*, April 1993, 58.

16. Louis Janssens, "Norms and Priorities of a Love Ethics," *Louvain Studies* 6 (Spring 1977): 216–23. Don Browning has used the Janssens perspective in an essay on "Altruism and Christian Love" in *Zygon* 27, no. 4 (December 1992): 421–36. For Browning, sacrifice is not the norm but a corrective that is necessary to restore the mutuality of love as equal regard.

17. *The Book of Common Prayer*, The Episcopal Church (New York: Seabury Press, 1979), 423.